INTRODUCTION TO WALLACE STEVENS

INTRODUCTION
TO
WALLACE
STEVENS

Henry W. Wells

1964

Indiana University Press

BLOOMINGTON

To
PATRICIA TERRY
Scholar, Translator,
Poet

Contents

Acknowledgment

I am grateful to the Estate of Wallace Stevens and to Alfred A. Knopf, Inc., the publisher of the poetry of Wallace Stevens, for permitting me to reprint from the following copyrighted editions: *The Collected Poems of Wallace Stevens* (1957), and *Opus Posthumous* (1957).

H.W.W.

INTRODUCTION TO WALLACE STEVENS

I : *Why a Companion to Wallace Stevens?*

IT WOULD be hard to exaggerate the unusual position occupied by Wallace Stevens in American poetry. Although he won for himself a high place in our literature during the years that witnessed the appearance of many eminent names in verse—Frost, Robinson, Eliot, Pound, Crane, Williams, and, possibly in a lower category, Elinor Wylie, Robinson Jeffers, E. E. Cummings, Allen Tate, Karl Shapiro, and a host of others—he belonged to no group and defied classification. Although it is clear that he knew English poetic rhetoric from Shakespeare to the present, that he possessed an intimate knowledge of French verse and had some command of the general field of European literature, none of his own writing is in the least imitative. Little in the earlier American poets influenced his own art, though he was much influenced by American thought and culture. His creative mind asserted itself in striking individuality and a rare degree of independence.

Literary society and professional men of letters he appeared rather to shun than to pursue. Working as a successful man of business, living in Hartford, Connecticut, a city of distinct cultural tradition but no great size or commanding position in the thought of the country, he stood apart and apparently relished his privacy. He avoided promiscuous conversation on literary topics, especially on whatever concerned his own work, so that even some of his intimates never knew him to be a writer. The publication of his first book he delayed. For several years discerning readers admired his poems appearing in periodicals and wondered who he was. He gave pleasure but remained to the world of letters something of a mystery. During the later part of his life, which extended to the full span of a man's years, he did, indeed, make a few public appearances and published some prose that in a measure explained his literary creed. But it is not too much to say that he continued to be a veiled figure almost to the end of his career and that the years following his death, in 1955, have only partially drawn aside these veils and placed his art and mind in a clearer light. To an unusual degree his reputation has been growing both steadily and surely.

The most casual glance at his pages shows that he possesses rare qualities. Though he by no means flaunts eccentricity or oddity of style and thought, as does that excellent poet, E. E. Cummings, likewise a New Englander with fresh turns of mind, Stevens' originality proves notably quiet and profound. He does not to any extent worth serious mention tease the bourgeoisie, after the manner of the American Bohemians or the European avant-garde, nor formally declare a new era in poetry, as do Eliot or Pound. He proposes no new laws for others; he merely cultivates new and fastidious standards for himself. It is not for any mannerisms that he is chiefly known, though, for example, the witty and often self-deprecatory titles chosen for his poems might be thought to reveal a mannerism. His originality runs much deeper than that.

Perhaps more than any other American poet of his times, he insists on the importance of intellectual thought in poetry and writes accordingly. Another of his leading principles of composition is compactness or "density" of expression, though this all-important principle in his writing he silently assumes and almost never mentions in his own critical observations. In his poetry is a maximum use of metaphor, symbolism, and general compactness; from this chiefly derives the "difficulty" of his expression. In a quiet way, to a degree exhibited by no other poet of his period, he affects what others proclaim: the creation of a new style or "language" for verse, one almost as far removed from the general idiom of communication as possible, although very frank, terse, and direct expressions, quite unrhetorical and unadorned and by no means uncolloquial, are occasionally found as one of the many features of his style. He is more thoughtful, imaginative, and elegant, not to mention eloquent, than most or possibly any of his contemporaries. Making understanding still more difficult, his works rise from his moods as well as from his mind and tongue and hence the reader of any of his poems must first of all discern by intuition and a sympathetic reading what the mood of any of his pieces may be. If from one point of view the poems are philosophical essays, from another they resemble musical compositions. They call for an approach that, if not essentially new, must nevertheless seem both fresh and somewhat elusive to the great majority of his readers and even to those best prepared to meet him on his own shifting grounds.

Stevens' works pose many problems and hand no ready key to his readers. Their variegated surface notwithstanding, they present a remarkably organic body of writing, from his earliest years to his last; few poems or pages of poems could be mistaken for those from another hand. To an exceptional degree certain thoughts and attitudes recur and even a fair number of symbols used in a personal manner are to be found. Occasionally one of his poems explicitly refers to another. The chief difficulty presented is not, however, a private or esoteric system but, on the contrary, that he is not a systematic thinker. Hence no formula guides us through the luxuriant labyrinth of his art and the paradoxes of his irony. A born ironist, he repeatedly writes poems that seem to contradict each other. He can be tragic or comic, grave or witty, gentle or harsh, sweet or acidulous, conservative or radical. His moods are almost Shakespearean in their infinite variety. Since many readers rely more than they are probably willing to admit on presuppositions, they find Stevens baffling: he confuses them for the really irrelevant reason that they cannot place him. This is as he should be, not as they should be. The explanation is simply that he is too large to be pocketed or pigeonholed. He writes with complete integrity, for the enlargement of his reader's heart, mind, and pleasure, not for the convenience of his reviewers, critics, or apologists.

In one highly important respect Stevens must seem not only elusive but virtually deceptive. In this regard, too, a prejudice may easily be formed. If his own repeated statements in his poems themselves are weighed literally and on their face value, it may appear that he is not the astonishingly versatile genius and free-playing mind which in actuality he is, but rather a narrow spirit chained to a single obsession. Much the greater part of his verse is to an important degree poetry about poetry. To such an extent does this aesthetic problem loom over him that it is not unfair to say that he writes poetry under an emotional compulsion which is also an intellectual compulsion: a need to explore the thesis that art is a supreme manner of grappling with reality. Stevens' mind is haunted by this metaphysical problem. How it became so engrossing to him will probably never be fully known, though doubtless much that is cogent and revealing in biography will in time be written. Such speculation by the intelligent and dedicated artist is certainly rationally justified. He seeks a rationale for his work, a mystique to warrant it in his own eyes. Most artists have had some warrant for their work at hand, as Shakespeare's lines on drama and acting, put into the mouth of Hamlet, so well indicate. But to be so far obsessed with this outlook that a large, possibly the largest, part of a poet's work grapples specifically with the subject, seems a species of mental and spiritual inversion, an almost incestuous relation between the poet and his productions. It suggests that he overlooks his audience, who have no such professional orientation, and speaks in soliloquy with himself. The condition looks unwholesome but insofar as it casts a blemish on Stevens' work, his times must share a part of the blame.

This is a very common condition in modern poetry. Fortunately there is no need to survey the full scope of the subject or to consider how much poetry, for example, of the eminent names mentioned earlier in this foreword falls within this category. Ezra Pound is forever pounding us with his ideas of art. T. S. Eliot's *Four Quartets* has art in its title and "the word" proves a large part of its subject matter. Hart Crane became a missionary for poetry, Elinor Wylie lamented her own servitude to words. William Carlos Williams' masterpiece, *Paterson*, deals in large measure with language and one part of the work, well-aired and unacademic as it is, is entitled "The Library." Karl Shapiro has written one long poem on the art of poetry and another devoted to Ezra Pound. The subject threatens endlessness. Its explanation is, doubtless, a virtually inescapable condition confronting the modern poet, self-conscious in his isolation from the general public, persuaded that he must carry the burden which theology has so recently laid aside, aware that he is talking in a new language by no means that of the market-place, and that he must in some measure justify his seeming eccentricity and explain to the masses of men, or even to his colleagues or to himself, what he is doing.

With Stevens the incentives seem even deeper than those indicated thus far. To all appearances he was born both a poet and a philosopher in aesthetics. Born, so to speak, a conjoined twin, he found himself in a difficult and occasionally embarrassing position. His poetry at times grew too philosophical and lost its spontaneity; his philosophy at times grew too vague and lost its cutting, rational edge. Divided within himself, he was all the more human in that he was not altogether a happy man. Here it must be added that finicky and almost affected as some of his early perfervid rhetoric appears, he is, in fact, one of the most lusty, robust, and firm-grained writers in

American literature, and perhaps the most gifted of all in expressing the joy of life. His thought can be either deeply comic or tragic. But a great streak, running bias like a fault over a face of rock, appears as a gash across his soul.

It should be remembered, however, that other poets, possibly greater than he, show such disproportion and disfeaturing. Undoubtedly Lucretius was a man haunted by an obsession, as fanatic in urging his atomic theory of the universe as Stevens in urging his metaphysical theories of art and imagination. The artist so conditioned is not invariably thwarted by his bias, though the man is almost always in some degree wounded. It may provide an irresistible impulse to composition, a fervor that the poet must at times share with the priest. For a lifetime Stevens was engaged in his priestly task of expounding the relations of art and reality. Of course it cannot be said that he solved the basic problems or even brought them into clear focus. But it can emphatically be said that in the course of his dedicated quest he created some of the finest poetry written in our century. His compulsion resembles the stem of a tree, his achievements in poetry may be likened to its fruits and flowers. To this image we must occasionally return in this book. Here lies one of the major problems for his careful reader. Overimpressed by Stevens' own description of his poems as essays in the theory of poetry, the reader too easily minimizes or even overlooks his deep humanity and comprehensive outlook on many phases of life that proliferate from this hard and at times almost repellent stem. The reader may well be unaccustomed to these conditions. He must, however, become at home with them if he is to begin the serious study and keener enjoyment of Stevens' poems.

In the perspective of general world literature the minor poets hardly deserve prolonged critical attention in print, though they may well receive such attention from that lugubrious gentleman, the literary historian. Any major poet deserves his critic, as, in Homer, any hero deserves his charioteer. But with Stevens the problem comes to more than that. Every reader worthy of the name cherishes his independence, his freedom from intrusion, his thoughtful solitude. Yet in the case of such a difficult and almost baffling poet as Stevens, who is nevertheless worthy of study almost in proportion to the degree of his difficulty, special conditions afford encouragement to the guide and interpreter. His art is to a surprising degree new, even in its peculiar blending of new and old. And new things almost always present stubborn obstacles.

As already indicated, such difficulties as this book may reasonably be expected to resolve are not minor difficulties or problems of detail. They much more nearly deserve the name, beloved by Stevens, of abstractions. The forms which his poetry assumes and the thoughts which it contains call for general comment; the poetry does not as a rule invite elucidation of detail. The scrutiny must, to be sure, be exceedingly close, often to an almost microscopic degree, but general conclusions, not masses of information, can alone throw light of any consequence upon the values of his art. Our study should avoid either platitudes on the general art of reading or problems so vexed and minute that their handling of detail must inevitably distort any general picture of Stevens' work. The problem is as unlike a crossword puzzle as possible; it is a question of style, psychology, habits of thought. This study holds as its foundation the assumption that the most elementary matters of reading in general are already resolved and that the most esoteric problems raised by Stevens need not concern us. It is assumed that careful and meticulous reading is the basis of all literary understanding, that such close-packed writing as Stevens' must receive this scrutiny, and that the reader has already reread the poems several times before examining the present book. Quotations, accordingly, will not be numerous, nor will any large number of Stevens' references or allusions be annotated.

His vocabulary is exceptionally large and his use of words precise, even fastidious. The better educated his reader is, the more often he is likely to consult a dictionary, but he will not need to do so often. This book does not propose to be a substitute for the dictionary. The further question of proper names raises a somewhat different problem, but here, too, little commentary need be expected. Stevens uses fewer allusions of this nature than many of his contemporaries in verse, fewer, I believe, than Eliot, and incomparably fewer than Pound, a writer peculiarly vain in airing his erudition. There are, perhaps, only a half dozen instances in all Stevens' works where a critic would seriously care to raise the question of possible pedantry, willful obscurity, or an artless personalism in allusions. Sometimes Stevens employs a proper name in a poem or title that might almost as well have been any other name. "From Havre to Hartford," he wrote once; but another French city would have done almost as well. The location of Havre probably weighs less with him than the alliteration. With a meticulous instinct for his art, he usually constructs each poem in such a manner that it shall be a self-explanatory microcosm. The exposition will presumably lie not upon the surface but within the framework of the poem. This book is essentially philosophical, not factual. Hard thought and a strenuous imagination are needed to extract the riches from Stevens' mines. The language may possibly appear dark in its imaginative style, but not to any serious degree in respect to its allusions or semantics.

The analysis of the poetry which is to follow deals chiefly with its content or, in other words, with its emotions and ideas. It is true that all art is manifest in nuances of expression; the artist's skill is in his command of his medium and that of the poet is, of course, in words. But here lies a major obstacle to all criticism: nuances almost by definition escape close analysis. The artist's *curiosa felicitas* too often begets the critic's laborious infelicity. Relatively little will be remarked in these pages on Stevens' remarkable verbal artistry as such. Yet something more than perfunctory notice must be taken of it and of his inspired rhetoric. In this regard attention may profitably turn to a few brilliant yet representative lines which may stand for the poet's style as a whole.

The style is richly sensuous, with deeply meaningful images drawn not only from hearing and seeing but from taste, touch, and smell. One does not require the context of the lines to recognize this quality. Since the reader, nevertheless, may wish to look them up, page references will be given, which, unless otherwise noted, refer to the *Collected Poems.* Where sound is concerned, take, for example, the lines: "The skreak and skritter of evening gone" (p. 160); "Heavenly labials in a world of gutterals" (p. 7); "With a blubber of tom-toms harrowing the sky" (p. 41); "The heavy bells were tolling rowdy-dow" (p. 155); "Bubbling felicity in cantilene" (p. 43); and, with silence having an effect of sound, "The holy hush of ancient sacrifice" (p. 67). Among the many eloquent references to music may be cited a passage in "Owl's Clover" (*Opus Posthumous*, p. 62):

> Then Basilawsky in the band-stand played
> "Concerto for Airplane and Pianoforte,"
> The newest Soviet reclame. Profound
> Abortion, fit for the enchanting of basilisks.

The eye of the imagination is chiefly invoked in a still greater number of lines, of which the following are representative: "She spoke with the backward gestures of her hand" (p. 435); "Blooming and beaming and voluming colors out" (p. 484); "By the consummation of the swallow's wings" (p. 68); "The spontaneities of rain or snow" ("Owl's Clover," *Opus Posthumous*, p. 67); "The necklace is a carving not a kiss" (p. 413); "Smacking their muzzy bellies in parade" (p. 59); "Gloomy grammarians in golden gowns" (p. 55); "Before these visible, voluble delugings" (p. 24); "All din and gobble, blasphemously pink" (p. 44), and "Is it a luminous flittering / Or the concentration of a cloudy day?" (p. 396). Of the many brilliant passages showing sculpture as the object seen one of the most memorable follows:

> The great statue of the General Du Puy
> Rested immobile, though neighboring catafalques
> Bore off the residents of its noble Place.
>
> The right, uplifted foreleg of the horse
> Suggested that, at the final funeral,
> The music halted and the horse stood still. (p. 391)

There will be other occasions to return to this unforgettable image.

The rich, sensuous, and imaginative language extends to the sense of smell. Of an August day it is said: "It is full of the myrrh and camphor of summer" (p. 490). The sensuous world would be incomplete without taste. In "Floral Decorations for Bananas" leaves of the banana plant are animated, so that we read of "Their musky and tingling tongues" (p. 54). Sensations of feeling are strongly evoked in a sentence with the words, "When the harmonious heat of August pines" (p. 399). Sometimes to the sensuous images is added a mysterious nuance that wholly escapes categorizing, except as *curiosa felicitas* itself. Consider, for instance, such lines as these: "In the grand decadence of the perished swans" (p. 145), and "Of the high interiors of the sea" (p. 5). With still greater distinction, Stevens achieves poetic eloquence without imagery, as in the phrase, "And there the soldier of time has deathless rest" (p. 319).

With a talent for abstraction quite different from that intended in Stevens' phrase, "it must be abstract," he attains a force unsurpassed by any sensuous image. The following are indicative: "The squirming facts exceed the squamous mind" (p. 215); "The hallaballo of health and have" (p. 292); "And the lost vehemence the midnights hold" (p. 72); "In the stale grandeur of annihilation" (p. 505); and "Parts of the immense detritus of a world" ("Owl's Clover," *Opus Posthumous*, p. 49). Let these lines suffice in the not unrewarding game of fishing for phrases or, to change the image, compiling an anthology of shining fragments. Quite another approach may prove even more useful.

The grandeur of any poet's achievement is best understood not in generalizations regarding his total work or his inspired phrases but in analysis of his chief works weighed individually. Economy of statement, however, encourages any interpreter to arrange his materials in terms of general ideas. In this connection a selective method is most rewarding. Poems are most profitably considered in the light of their outstanding characteristics; some, for example, shine especially in terms of their form or lyric expression, some are notable for peculiarities of style, for philosophical content, humor or fantasy, psychological or emotional weight, an epic spirit, or for imaginative commentary on organized society. The discussion of Stevens' poems naturally envisages certain groupings of them. In all, over a hundred poems will be examined in some detail, discussions falling into approximately a dozen categories. To many other poems, naturally, allusions will be made. If we can find our way to somewhere near the bottom of these pieces, it seems unlikely that serious difficulties will confront us with any others. Some selection is almost inevitable on the critic's part, as some repetition is inevitable even in the pages of the most imaginative poet of whatever time or land.

In conclusion, a few more specific words should be said regarding the poems discussed or omitted from discussion. The criterion has been in general their representative value, although what is assumed to be the relative merit of the pieces has also been considered. In other words, the poems chiefly studied are deemed both the best and most typical of Stevens' poetic accomplishment. The title of this book is by no means accidental. It is designed as an introduction to a most difficult and yet most rewarding body of literary material or, one might prefer to say, treasure. Some of Stevens' poems are so simple and direct as to discourage exegesis, just as in a few he becomes so far entangled in his subtleties that exegesis would in the end prove more laborious than profitable. In a number of cases he follows, at least roughly, certain formulas which, if examined in one instance, may be mastered for all.

Economy has argued against a detailed study of several of his longer poems, to which references are made but which have not invited detailed interpretation. For several reasons these pieces have been given subordinate or almost negligible attention. The early and brilliant "Comedian as the Letter C" is, unlike most of its author's works, graced with a straightforward narrative, so that it is less in need of explanatory comment. True, its highly rhetorical or ornamented style occasionally leads Stevens into something of a snarl. But these few darkened passages hardly demand special comment here. "The Comedian as the Letter C" differs from most of Stevens' works in that it seems clearer than it is, whereas his most mature long poems are really clearer and more strictly organized than they at first appear. Two long and important pieces not to be treated in detail, "Notes toward a Supreme Fiction" and "An Ordinary Evening in New Haven," are superficially glossed partly because they repeat much to be found in still finer poems, as "Esthétique du Mal," partly because they are somewhat drier and more subject to the charge of naked intellectualism than most of Stevens' best work, and finally because, owing to their advanced intricacies of statement, they should be read last among his works and not first. No one who has read carefully "Esthétique du Mal" and "Owl's Clover," both examined here with special care, should find any serious difficulty in reading such poems as "Notes toward a Supreme Fiction," "An Ordinary Evening in New Haven," "The Rock," and a handful of comparable works.

Stevens wrote a few poems of considerable length that may be described as verse essays or odes and a large number of short poems. This book begins at once with an analysis of one of his finest long poems, "Esthétique du Mal," and concludes with an analysis of an equally fine but quite different long poem, "Owl's Clover." Toward the center of the book will be examined three unusually substantial and especially artful poems of considerable complexity and moderate length and somewhat similar form and content, "Chocorua to Its Neighbor," "Transport to Summer," and "The Auroras of Autumn." In the intervening spaces poems of various length but for the most part rather short will be considered, with the convenience that Stevens, who possessed almost unique powers for saying much in little, says in these pieces what he has to say generally with as much succinctness and clarity as the subtleties of his ideas and feelings admit. The entire arrangement is designed to offer the most practical interpretive introduction to Stevens' avowedly difficult but remarkably rewarding poetry. One might almost assert that with him the more arduous the climb, the more splendid the view. On reaching the summit we forget the effort, delighted with the panorama. Evaluations, though freely admitted, are nowhere developed at length. "Three Travelers Watch a Sunrise" is, for example, in my opinion a much more important play than it has ever been described to be, but the view will not be urged at length here. Stevens' strong personal characteristics notwithstanding, he must, I think, be commended for a greater scope than that of T. S. Eliot, dominated by the opposing spirits of frustration and reconciliation, or that of W. B. Yeats, with his gyres, his violence, and his antitheses, or Edith Sitwell, with her masks of fantasy and devotion. In elegance he is unsurpassed. But this study is primarily interpretive. On the basis of an interpretation that will be a collaboration between the views offered here, insights from other sources, and his own, the reader is encouraged to evaluate the poems as he will. I am fully confident that on the whole he will value them highly and that an increasingly favorable estimate of them will be held by the public for many years to come.

11 : *A Long Philosophical Elegy, in Strophes*

THAT considerable effort is required of the reader of Wallace Stevens' poetry appears most clearly in his longer works, partly for the obvious reason that the effort necessarily becomes more sustained. These complex works also are in every sense his most ambitious creations, most strongly demanding the reader's exertions. Whether his contributions to poetry are intrinsically greater in his longer or shorter works is a hard question, scarcely calling for a categorical answer. Certainly as author of dozens of short poems of lyric spirit, notably in his first volume, *Harmonium*—for example, such pieces as "The Paltry Nude Starts on a Spring Voyage"—he shows remarkable lyrical gifts. But as the years advanced, he composed a fair number of works extending to two hundred lines or more. The second edition of *Harmonium* itself contained a poem of approximately six hundred lines, "The Comedian as the Letter C." Of course, any evaluations must be relative, if only because there is no generally received notion as to how long a long poem must be. One reader might consider "Sunday Morning," in its final version with a hundred and twenty lines, as a long poem; another might require considerably more lines than that. In any case, Stevens invites some distinction between two categories, wherever one may prefer to draw the line. The really significant difference consists in quality rather than size. A long poem for Stevens generally implies an elaborately protracted argument, since he is an intellectual as well as a poet. But intellect moves more slowly than emotion. Hence the tendency of the brief poem, unless, perhaps, it be a witty epigram, is to be emotional or, better, intuitive; the long poem, at least in his hands, is endowed with considerable intellectual content. Almost all his poems, no matter how brief, have some reflective element. But his more extended works tend to become in a sense philosophical essays, in this respect resembling Alexander Pope's major poems. Thought, not narrative or anecdote, impelled Stevens to length of utterance.

Although a narrative element is present in "The Comedian as the Letter C," this poem, written in blank verse, traces the development of a style rather than the adventures of one or more persons. "Sunday Morning," though a considerably briefer work, is more representative of the poet's manner in most of his longer poems, the majority of which bear a resemblance to the classical ode disposed in strophes—for there is much more lyrical afflatus in Stevens than in Pope. The spirit of the essay in blank verse, to be sure, appears in "Owl's Clover" and a few other pieces; but as a rule Stevens' longer poems are arranged in more or less regular strophes, which, with a touch of originality, he presents as individual poems in a closely knit sequence. His exacting sense of form leads him at times to subdivide the strophes into lesser sections. The

triplet appeals to him most, though in "The Man with
the Blue Guitar" he uses the couplet, doubtless because
whoever strums the guitar plays an instrument with a relatively low resonance. Such matters are of considerable concern to the reader, for always the understanding or full
enjoyment of a poem by Stevens calls for a close observation of its form as technique. His manner in this regard
is as a rule leisurely; a sonnet sequence might have seemed
to him, among its other limitations, short-winded. The
strophes in "Sunday Morning" have fifteen lines. In several cases a sequence of twenty lines or more is maintained. Similarly, his pronounced gift for rhetoric led to
a highly successful cultivation of the verse paragraph in
the baroque or neo-Miltonic manner, as in "The Comedian as the Letter C." With more imaginative pressure
behind them, the magnificent paragraphs of that poem
and of "Owl's Clover," all montages in the baroque style,
are transformed into the strophes of his more typical
works, revealing an affinity with music and dancing.

All his work is rewarding but not all in equal measure.
The major poem as he conceived it tempted him to develop his intellectual acumen perilously close to the risk
of his aesthetic inspiration. Thus "The Man with the
Blue Guitar" may be more witty than profound; "Notes
toward a Supreme Fiction," though justly admired, possibly impinges at times upon prose; and "An Ordinary
Evening in New Haven" carries intellectual dryness to
such an extreme that the doctrine of austerity which it
appears to defend may become doctrinaire and the approach be suspected of didacticism. Though such works
are substantial, they are also a bit heavy. The finest creations of poetry, like the best products of the kitchen, need

not and should not be heavy. They must be supported by an address to the feelings as well as to the mind and by a direct address to the poetic imagination. Almost all Stevens' poems, long or short, are more or less concerned with aesthetics, or with the philosophy of the imagination. These problems are to him the problems not merely of the artist but of life itself. The critique of art he views as the critique of life. It is not necessary, he holds, that all persons read poetry or write it, but it is necessary for a good life that they should breathe this freer air and think in this larger domain. Unimaginative people are for Stevens only half alive. Our modern world, he holds, is threatened with serious decay of the imagination. He regards himself as both poet and seer, both creator and, in his own use of the word, "rabbi." In some of his pages the seer and rabbi take the wind from the sails of the poet and creator. He becomes orotund and oratorical. As previously observed, he presents his critic with a problem roughly analogous to that posed by Lucretius, who as a rule uses a philosophy of nature with great purpose for his art but occasionally allows the thinker to supersede the poet, much as Stevens uses the philosophy of aesthetics, or of the poetic imagination, with similar results. Stevens is never the sentimentalist; on the contrary, at times he becomes the pundit of an argument extremely finespun, recondite, and conceivably arid.

In "Esthétique du Mal" such temptations are largely overcome by an exceptionally fortunate orientation toward direct experience, for the poem is at once highly intellectual and deeply felt. The thought arises from tragic experience. The poem is austere and, in a very different degree, an analysis of it must be austere also. Clearly, some violent experience, a bereavement and a grief, is assumed to lie behind the lines, as anterior action lies behind the first scenes of a classical tragedy or behind any of its choral odes. The problems of creative imagination are applied to an event no less real because it remains unspecified. We read of the wound of the individual and of the wounds of soldiers, of private and public grief, but it is also made clear that all grief is essentially private, just as all grief conceived by the creative imagination by virtue of this act itself becomes public. As its title states and its contents confirm, "Esthétique du Mal," like almost all Stevens' major poems, deals with aesthetics. Yet this work is, with several of his shorter and more lyrical pieces, also an elegy, designed for the unknown and unspecified soldier in time of war and for the unspecified civilian at all times. To use Stevens' own formula of expression, his poem might have been called "The Tragedian as the Letter T." It deals not only, as does "Sunday Morning," with a theory of the emotional life but with the realization of it in semi-dramatic terms. It is a highly philosophical elegy, concerned with the greatest of all evils in any time, that of a violent bereavement, but explicitly with this evil as it confronts the modern man. Stevens is almost always highly conscious of both time and place. He possesses, as his thinking shows in general and such a poem as "Owl's Clover" reveals in particular, a profound historical imagination. By the same token, he is sharply aware of being himself a modern, addressing a contemporary audience in terms of its own problems and conditions. These considerations define the felicitously chosen theme of this major poem, in which he clearly exerts his energies to the full. The reader must realize, the title notwithstanding, that it is truly an elegy and moreover a new type of elegy, fashioned within the consciousness of a new age.

This is a poem to be read slowly, carefully, and, needless to say, repeatedly. On the twentieth reading we may think that we have squeezed its meaning dry but in truth it is inexhaustible. It is one of the few poems to which one can always return encouraged with confidence that an imaginative scrutiny will yield new riches. The following analysis of its form and meaning is not, of course, offered as comprehensive but only as, in view of the poem's profundity, useful. Perhaps Stevens cannot be wholly absolved of the charge of being needlessly obscure. He may even at times be a slovenly thinker, though it is difficult to support such a charge. In general, the metaphorical style and the compressed expression fully justify themselves.

Even for Stevens, "Esthétique du Mal" appears to have been written under an extraordinarily happy dominance of the poetic imagination. In form it is neither loose, as his poetry seldom proves to be, nor over-rigid, as it appears at time to become. One cannot well speak of stanzas here but rather of strophes. The individual sections, of which there are fifteen, ranging from twenty-one to twenty-six lines, possess too much independence to be regarded merely as stanzas. They are, to repeat, more like individual poems strung together in a sequence, as a sequence of philosophical sonnets. Yet the sections are imaginatively presented as a unified whole. The argument is, perhaps, rather circuitous but it can be followed. It is distinctly more thoughtfully designed than the analogous arguments in "The Man with the Blue Guitar" or "An Ordinary Evening in New Haven."

The basic argument is that grief, evil, or, more specifically, bereavement, can be endured if conceived by the poetic imagination or an imagination analogous to it. The poem does not deal with the techniques of art, which seldom, if ever, concern Stevens as subject matter in his poetry, as they concerned Karl Shapiro as his *Essay on Rime*. Stevens habitually deals with larger, distinctly metaphysical problems of the imagination. His approach in this poem concerns chiefly the relation between art and tragic emotion. Here he concludes, with an emphasis not always found in his work, which is at times primarily witty, that deep feeling is the essential subject matter of the serious artist and that art and poetry themselves exist first of all not for light entertainment but as aids, even therapeutic aids, enabling man to surmount his tragic predicament. The view is really a familiar one, eloquently stated all the way from Aristotle's prose to Emily Dickinson's verse. But Stevens introduces many considerations less commonly stated and perhaps quite as important as his major contention. In the last strophe he presents the thought that the services of a hedonistic outlook, wise in accepting the good of the physical world, may well accompany the more austere realization of tragic catharsis in establishing human life on a normal and happy footing.

In this connection it should be observed that Stevens has been too often described as a comic philosopher, as Robert Pack describes him, and identified with the outlook so clearly presented in "The Comedian as the Letter C." True, he is almost certainly our most urbane and sophisticated poet. But he plumbs tragic depths as well, as "Esthétique du Mal" so distinctly shows. Here another of his poems may be cited. "The Owl in the Sarcophagus" bears a title ambiguous as to its seriousness, but the poem is in fact a tender and sensitive analysis of the emotions of a bereaved person in the modern world. As with so many of Stevens' poems of eminently serious content, the title carries a touch of self-satire and even frivolity. The practice serves as a shield to discourage the sentimentalist and guard the breast of the supersensitive and really over-emotional poet. It is also a spell to ward off pomposity. The title "Esthétique du Mal" is itself in some respects a variant of this practice, concealing an elegy under the cloak of a homily. The first lines describe a smoldering volcano that is actually the poet himself. "Esthétique du Mal" is a stronger poem than "The Owl in the Sarcophagus" partly because it is more dramatic and less impressionistic, richer in ideas and more flexible in mood. It is flexible almost to the point of being bewildering. There are times, to repeat, when even the most experienced reader may not resent the services of a guide from step to step of its ascent.

The first strophe presents disaster in the image of a volcano, but indicates that even so great a menace may, with the aid of a classical discipline, be viewed more or less dispassionately and objectively, as when it is seen in the corner of a mirror, or when one reflects that conscious pain so far as man is aware is virtually reserved for man alone: nature herself is sublime in unfeeling. The imagery includes the portrait of a man at Naples writing a letter home; here the delicate inference is that his letter concerns personal grief but that a certain distance lies between the cause of the sorrow and him who experiences it. Very simply, one must somehow survive pain. Life must go on.

Strophe two, less stocked with intellectual distinctions, considers the exhilarating or healing properties of the physical world, which at the hour of the sharpest grief are wholly forgotten but which, after the self-exhaustion of a passionate sorrow, may and should come as natural alleviation. Not alone lofty thought or art, abstraction or beauty, save life from despair; sensuous well-being and gratification have their alleviating functions as well. Stevens is an aristocrat of the mind, a democrat of the heart. He is fastidious but no prig, refined but remarkably robust.

Romantic excesses, as commonly found in Christianity, receive attention in the third strophe, which contrasts the agony of a forced asceticism with the simpler hedonism painted in strophe two. Our Christian God has been over-human, or, to state the case more clearly, too much given to pity, the blood-brother of self-pity. The strophe is especially thought-provoking; it is also written with deep compassion, though the familiar Christian compassion is called to account.

The error which is the obverse of cosmic pity is cosmic optimism or any indiscriminate spreading of a confident emotion throughout life. The thought is ingeniously and imaginatively developed. The title of a botanical volume, "Livre de Toutes Sortes de Fleurs d'après Nature," is offered as symbol of the indiscriminate mind caught in the meshes of the emotional life. Antithetical to this incipient pantheism is the concentration of music, which in the hands of the great formalists, as Bach, Beethoven, and Brahms, focuses upon a final chord, wherein one note seems dominant. Or, to employ another image, Stevens alludes to a Spanish poet, possibly Gongora, who selects the rose as a comprehensive symbol. The sum of this argument, for a time a little difficult to follow, is that man should by no means shun the deepest concentration of emotion in love or friendship. He should on no account attempt to avoid emotional stress but rather should work his way through it, making sure, as already explicitly stated, that his emotions are not wasted either in undue pity or in sentimental dilution.

The fifth strophe describes true emotion in terms of sincere expression, tender words spoken possibly with repetition but certainly without flatulent rhetoric, distracting attention from the experience itself to the gilded word. Religion, Stevens continues, once gave our most adequate formulas for the most emotional expressions, formulas which the secularity of the modern world must unhappily dispense with. Hence the extremes of baroque rhetoric are outmoded and windy; poignant simplicity and directness better agree with the modern temper. Here Stevens illustrates his thought with some of the most poignant words which he ever wrote, which should really be read in context, not quoted: "Be near me, come closer, touch my hand." Stevens' tragic sense argues for inwardness as against externality, for what he terms "in-bar" as opposed to "ex-bar."

He has now reached the heart of his subject, the hard core of evil and pain which must be confronted because it cannot in the long run possibly be escaped. He uses an image in itself more gorgeous and baroque than philosophically definitive but in the manner of the strongest mythological poetry. The sixth strophe is both primitive and Asiatic. In several poems he finds in golden fruit, as well as in the sun, a light-symbol of well-being and in the depredations of a sharp-beaked bird an image for universal

malice, evil, and destruction. Has he, perhaps, seen a tou-
can assaulting its food? His metaphor further suggests the
Vishnu-Siva imagery of life and death. A notable instance
of the bird-image is the short and early poem, "The Bird
with the Coppery, Keen Claws." The strophe in "Esthétique du Mal" is a Blakean evocation, much enhancing
the color and poetic splendor of the poem, making the
thought more vivid without retarding its movement un-
duly. The passage is essential to the poem's progress and
free from indulgence in the intellectual overtones rendering so many parts of it elusive. Its reader will grasp the
strophe *in toto* or not at all. This is a poem in itself. It
should be noted that the "clownish yellow" of the sun is
regarded as essentially an illusion: life is here conceived
as at bottom tragic, not comic.

The following strophe, employing the imagery of war,
plunges its reader into the heart of Stevens' tragedy. For
the twentieth century, war provides the supreme symbol,
or rather instance, of both death and evil. Stevens, as always, erects a projection of the concrete to bridge the path
to the abstract. Nothing can be more concrete than the
red wound of the individual soldier, nothing more general
than the thought of all wounded soldiers in all wars. Thus
the strophe exquisitely balances the abstract and the specific. As image for the general, Stevens employs one of his
favorite symbols, the mountain. In the vastness of the universe, suggested by the mountain, the soldier finds "deathless rest." Life's problem is of the one and the many, the
one as hero ennobled by his service to the many, the many
ultimately significant only in terms of the individual, who
stands always beneath his apex of the sky. Hence the Dantesque image of the fixed figures on an eternally moving

wheel. The painful experience of the wound must be healed by an imaginative grasp of the universal. But this in turn hinges upon the most personal tenderness. Stevens imagines a bereaved woman smoothing her forehead with her hand and thus soothing the soldier's wound. The meaning, of course, is that the grief here considered is defined not in terms of the dead, who are no longer conscious, but in terms of the living. The reality of death is the thought of death, resolved in the minds and hearts of the bereaved. This strophe is written at Stevens' height of warm inspiration.

The next section, strophe eight, is cast in more specifically intellectual terms. Evil for Stevens is conceived as Satanic. With Satan came death into the world and all its ill. Hence an analysis of the conception of Satan has basic significance in Stevens' by no means heretical description of death and evil. But, observes the poet, modern man no longer believes either in Satan or in sin. Yet the world is no less evil than when sin was acknowledged and Satan held a reality; and, obviously, death is with us still. Mythology and poetry once provided a weapon and shield for mankind warring against evil. But now men must clearly have a new weapon and a new defense. We find ourselves in a quandary. A superficial sophistication, with an outlook impossible to justify or sustain, prefers as far as possible to overlook all evil and all moral responsibility and similarly to gloss lightly over the existence of pain. But this evasion is simpy not viable. In reality, men are possibly more pained and beleaguered by their consciousness of guilt than ever. Such are the prosaic commonplaces behind Stevens' far from commonplace strophe. As champion of the poetic imagination, his first impulse is to deplore the absence of adequate and spontaneous poetry and religion, to acknowledge that the gods are now ghosts, and to lament their decline into this phantasmal limbo. Then, arresting his own romantic flight into the world of phantasms, he laments the bewilderment of the modern realist, or truth-seeker. More penetratingly, he realizes that less has changed than appears to have changed and that most of the old problems are with us still in new guises. The strophe is remarkably aphoristic. Stevens' declaration that "the death of Satan was a tragedy for the imagination" has, in fact, often been quoted. But higher qualities of poetry than an aphoristic style reside in the lines, as in the observation that Satan's death "had nothing of the Julian thundercloud: the assassin flash and rumble."

With loss of mythology comes a loss to the imagination. The literalness induced by modern science tends to replace the poetry implicit in folklore. We think pragmatically and prosaically. With images highly precise and more than merely eloquent, Stevens in strophe nine deplores the loss of sensibility and fancy. He observes, however, that quite as in the case of morality, the degree of innovation is readily exaggerated—modern art and imagination seem infatuated under the spell of the neo-primitive. The emotions and their imaginative expression return all the more tempestuously for having been retarded. Under the guidance of Stravinsky and Picasso, whom Stevens does not name here but whom he certainly recalls, we desire "a primitive ecstacy." "Esthétique du Mal" repeats the thought found in his earlier "Sunday Morning."

The next strophe explains and defends modern sensuality as needful for our grasp of reality. With a romantic turn of thought, Stevens defends it further in terms of an "innocence" which relieves us from oppressive dogmas. The strophe is highly symbolic, woven about an image of warm and fecund maternity. It may well owe some of its sentiment to Renoir.

Yet however much modern man seeks the solace of sensuality, and possibly on this very account, he is forced back to confront life's essential bitterness. Strophe eleven states this problem with reversion to the major theme of the aesthetic imagination, which requires the sensuous world and in its purity rejects all temptations to sentimentality or dishonest art, or, better, which savors both false and true expression in order to prefer the latter. The beauty of art grows without decadence, even out of the decadence of man. Here, as elsewhere in the poem, Stevens was probably thinking of Baudelaire.

Strophe twelve is an extraordinary and possibly a dubious *tour de force*. Among other considerations, Stevens seems to have offered it in vivid contrast to the preceding encomium upon "the most grossly maternal," the earlier strophe being a celebration of sensuousness, the later a witty extravaganza in intellectual fencing. The poet's love for dialectic here determines his style, reducing it to an extreme dryness. Doubtless there is a vigorous pleasure in such scholastic argumentation. But the brilliance of the debate actually darkens its meaning; the style may be aesthetic, in the sense of a thing of joy and beauty; it is hardly forthright statement.

Translated for convenience' sake into more readily intelligible terms, the meaning is virtually as follows—with the reservation that no paraphrase can be precise. In Stevens' eyes the problem of sentimentality voiced in the preceding strophe weighs less for modern civilization than the dilemma stated in this: our schizophrenic world he envisages as split between the problems of the community and the individual. What we have so recently learned and discovered about ourselves falls into two imperfectly reconciled domains, those of sociology and psychology. Pursuing this line of thought with a flourish of logic, Stevens argues that we must know others through ourselves or ourselves through others, neither procedure giving assurance of truth. In less abstract terms than employed by Stevens, the argument points to frustration in both personal and political life. We live beneath two ailing systems of thought most strikingly represented by Marx and Freud, neither adequate in its own terms and the two taken together leaving us in a divided and most imperfect world. Furthermore, when all rational search for truth or reality is discarded, evil itself must be dissolved in the general vapidity. It ceases to be a reality. Yet, logic to the contrary, every man, and especially every woman, knows it in fact as only too real.

In strophe thirteen some further possible solutions are suggested. The Calvinistic doctrine of inherited evil, though supported by much modern experiment and learning, is rejected. Viewed here only with a certain mild tolerance is the attitude of common sense, whereby the urbane Western mind, of Mediterranean origin, discovers the solid good in life at least possibly to outweigh its undeniable ill.

The passages immediately foregoing, as Stevens himself suggests, are subject to the suspicion of sophistry; reasoning may appear sound and even be so within its own premises and yet in the end be scarcely better than lunacy. Can "the politics of the emotion," asks the poet in strophe fourteen, be safely arbitrated by reason? Interestingly enough, he quotes Victor Serge's remark to this effect concerning Konstantinov. With no violent transition the thought turns next to Geneva, its philosophers and metaphysicians, who debated so audaciously regarding evil and sin. Contemplated in one of the moods in which Stevens is thoroughly at home, the magnificent speculations of these thinkers resemble the intangible splendor of clouds, having little relation to actual living, like the swaying of some ponderous curtains. Is his own poem, too, something like this? He gives, as it were, a poetic and sophisticated transcription of the familiar aphorism that philosophers have their heads in the clouds. The strophe is moving and singularly undogmatic.

The conclusion of the poem, in strophe fifteen, again advances a defense of a sensuous life and a still warmer and more discriminating defense of the imaginative life, which to be valid must itself reconcile demands of the physical and the abstract. Most miserable, says Stevens, uniting the minor and the major themes of his poem, is the "logical lunatic," or, indeed, anyone who in his folly has lost contact with the world of matter. This, as he has earlier observed, must, with the help of art, save him in the end, if saved he will be. The poem's conclusion provides no melodramatic surprises, for it has been assumed from its beginning. The writer observing Vesuvius in strophe one is clearly the artist, and strophe two clearly states the healing powers of nature herself as companioned by art. Life is in the end bearable not so much because it is found good in ethical terms as because it is found magnificent both to the naïve and the most highly trained aesthetic eye, various as men are various and, as Miranda discovered it, indubitably wonderful.

There is little new in Stevens' final words of wisdom yet they are supported by great imaginative power in both thought and art. He has composed a modern elegy dealing warmly and sympathetically with the emotional life, though a classical discipline and restraint stands high among his desiderata. "Esthétique du Mal," though not technically a tragedy, is a powerful tragic poem, in essence an ode of Sophoclean beauty and one of the major poems in American literature, along with masterpieces such as "When Lilacs Last in the Dooryard Bloomed," "The Waste Land," "Paterson," and "The Bridge." Its place of merit within Stevens' own poetry becomes to some extent a matter of personal choice. Readers hospitable to lavish introduction of the intellect in poetry will possibly prefer it to "Sunday Morning;" those fearful of such intrusion may even prefer a casual reading of Stevens' miracle of sensuous beauty, "Sea Surface Full of Clouds." "Esthétique du Mal" lacks the dramatic force of several of his earlier lyrics. Yet within the domain of philosophical poetry it must seem unusually warm and even tender, though its fire burns beneath the surface and much of its tenderness is expressed by hints in place of insistence. Elusive but not irrelevant, it provides a remarkable variant on the classical conception of the personal elegy. Its last stanza, which in some respects follows the thought of the book of Job, provides the excellent advice that man does best not to blame nature for his ills but to look to himself.

Much of the best of Stevens, with the exception of his ironic wit and lyric grace, is here. A reader wrestling seriously with his intricate art and fine-spun thought can hardly do better than concentrate upon "Esthétique du Mal," for this is work as typical as it is rewarding. Stevens' long poem closest to it in merit and packed meaning is the satirical "Owl's Clover," cast in a distinctly different vein, a poem to be examined in the last few pages of this volume. But any reader who has mastered the elements in the appreciation of "Esthétique du Mal" may approach with much confidence any item, short or long, in the ample and varied body of Wallace Stevens' poetry.

III : *Forms of Poetry*

O F THE total of Stevens' poetry thus far published, considerably more than a third falls into the category including "Esthétique du Mal," namely, the long poem as this is commonly regarded, or the poem of substantially over a hundred lines. Most of these major works can be described as belonging to the familiar genre of verse essay. They are usually reflective poems comparable to elegies in the classical or neo-classical tradition. When most inspired and truly the poet, as in "Esthétique du Mal," Stevens composes poetry transcending the verse essay and more nearly resembling the ode. But many of his longer productions, closely written and brilliant as they are, remain in a realm not far removed from meditative prose. They may be compared with Thomas Traherne's *Centuries of Meditations,* or possibly with John Dryden's powerful but didactic and intellectual verse. The long poems are eminently substantial. A subjective estimate, but one not likely to be disputed, is that they uphold the high level of his work as a whole without conspicuously surpassing it. As previously observed, only two of the repre-

37

sentative long poems are analyzed in detail in this book, namely, the elegiac "Esthétique du Mal" and the philosophical and satirical "Owl's Clover." These are masterpieces of their kind. Yet nine times out of ten it is to the Stevens of the short poems that allusion is made and by these he is certainly best remembered. It is with these briefer works that the immediately following pages deal.

Assisted above all by his acute ear and his sprightliness, both natural and cultivated, as well as by his feeling for music and the dance, he wrote many works that in the more extensive understanding of the term can indisputably be called lyrical. Such poems are generally unconventional lyrics and to this extent invite commentary. But they are at least basically lyrical, ranging from longer and more formal pieces resembling short choral odes to brief and spontaneous pieces resembling airs. In a writer of Stevens' strong metaphysical and intellectual bent this genuinely lyric vein appears somewhat surprising. With a musical rhythm in his mind, he developed short poems of unmistakably musical inspiration. The imagery and movement likewise often betray the rhythm of dancing feet.

Despite the obsessive attraction which aesthetic doctrine held for Stevens, he possessed the breadth of mind and power of imagination to achieve much versatility. His deep insight into almost all arts and areas of aesthetics, his knowledge and appreciation not only of music and dance but of sculpture, architecture, painting, and the decorative arts as well, greatly aided this skill in the lyric and the short poem generally. A core-image often relates a short poem to a still-life painting. The subect-matter of the poem contracts to a single theme or its imagery appears rigidly bounded by the dimensions of a relatively small canvas. Formulas based on theme and variation control a considerable number of pieces. In addition, he cultivates still other modes, as the verse aphorism, light verse, weighty or sprightly satire, and, as if to show that he *could* do what he so seldom saw fit to do, on one or two occasions he approximates narrative form. Although he seldom had use for them, he knew the italics of dramatic effect. He even composed two highly unorthodox and memorable little plays, one with at least a strong suggestion of opera or cantata, the other, with notable elements from the modern dance. These plays have been relatively neglected by the public and the critics, as have Stevens' achievements in his various categories of the short poem. The man, his ideas, and, above all, his style, have usurped attention, but he appears much more approachable and inviting when his command of these familiar forms of poetry is closely observed.

One of his most impressive poems of lyric inspiration, "Dutch Graves in Bucks County," has for Stevens an unusually pronounced lyric formula. It consists in twelve five-line stanzas, after each of which are two lines resembling a chorus, or refrain. The entire poem is seen as a meditation within the mind of the poet; the five-line stanzas primarily depict the condition of modern warfare, the only exception being stanza nine, where the masses of modern fighters become passingly aware of the subjects of the twelve choral couplets. These are dedicated to the Dutch dead, religious colonists in the New World, who for generations have rested quietly in their graves. Now the tumults of modern war overhead rouse them fitfully from their slumbers. Their ghost-like voices contrast their

own archaic days with the darkened era of world war.
Religious freedom propelled them to the New World.
Man, says the poet, must in the end find new freedoms
from war after the disasters which its ravages reveal to all
men. For eight couplets the supernatural voices recognize
only the vast distances separating their archaic past from
the turbulent present. Gradually, however, a consciousness dawns on them that in occult fashion the new and
necessary quest of the freedom from war which must at
long last follow the devastations of modern warfare is itself related to the doctrine of personal freedom, encouraged, says Stevens, in those quaint old Protestant congre-
gations.

Although no actual refrain is formulated, the more or
less uniform character of the couplets gives the impression of choral writing and of a refrain. The poem becomes
a chanted dialogue between the living soldiers and the
dead, the new and old, one chant comparatively rotund
and loud, the other whispered and ghost-like. (There is
a suggestion here of Thomas Hardy's ghost-haunted
poetry.) All this is typical of Stevens' synthetic mind,
equally impressed by past and present. But the poem
proves much subtler than has so far been indicated and
also still more firmly in the lyrical mode. There are significant crescendoes and variations. By virtue of the imagery,
the commotion wrought by the modern soldiers, with
their noisy airplanes and their clanking tread, grows louder
and louder, nearer and nearer to us, and ever more menacing, from the first through the fifth stanza. The sixth
stanza marks the chief advance of the poem as a work of
intellect: the assertion that modern warfare must at last
consume itself and turn toward peace. The seventh evokes

the frail image of still another army, that of the Confederacy, which swept like a storm across the fields of Pennsylvania only to retire and disperse itself in total defeat. This suggestion broadens the poem's scope, fixing a mark midway between the extremes of the two groups constituting its major concerns and developing a tragic underplot equally devoted to the military theme.

The voice of the modern army surges upward again in the ninth stanza. With a surprising turn, in this stanza the living soldiers hear, or think they hear, what they imagine to be the irrelevant pitter-patter of the ghostly voices. The three succeeding stanzas and their accompanying refrains gradually turn the tide of this indecisive and phantom-ridden dialogue to the advantage of the past. The soldiers of the present march toward a resolution of their problem without knowing that they are so doing, indeed, without even envisaging their problem. The ghostmen at last realize that they have not lived in vain, that their love of a spiritual freedom has sown seeds for future harvests. The poet, whose comments are deftly woven into the whole, shows an impartiality but a certain hopefulness regarding the modern men and a distinct liking for these Pennsylvania Dutch ancestors, the men of peace as opposed to those of war. Even among Stevens' poems this is conspicuous for its tenderness and sustained lyric beauty.

We have noted that his success in the lyric manner derives in considerable measure from his appreciation of music and dancing, as his minor poems conspicuously show. It would not be excessive to say that they reveal even some technical knowledge of music. The poems make reference to composers both classical and modern,

as Mozart and the modern Russians, and especially to
music for the keyboard instruments, the clavier and piano,
in whose literature the poet was something of a connoisseur. The spirit of music, its rhythms and formal patterns,
passes naturally into his own compositional style as an
artist in words. As convenient instance may be cited two
poems based in part on the rhythm of nursery songs, "Cortège for Rosenbloom," and "Ploughing on Sunday." The
first is such a wry, witty march tune as Haydn might have
composed. The miniature procession at the burial of the
rose, which is the poem's theme, also strongly suggests
the famous ballet, La Spectre de la Rose, one of Nijin-
sky's most famous dances, with music by Karl Maria
von Weber. But the poem is rather a ceremonial and
processional march than a dance. The strongly stressed,
rigidly repetitive words and rhythms express the merciless
march of the insects carrying off the corpse of the rose
"to a chirr of gongs and a chitter of cries and the heavy
thrum of the endless tread." The spirit seems more that
of the realist Moussorgsky than of the romanticist von
Weber; the poet is more concerned with the body of his
heroine than with her specter. It would be hard to find
any poem conveying better the impression of the music
of a march. Stevens has solved a problem too often left
unsolved. The words have in themselves a strong meaning
and a deeply appealing imagery. This is poetry, the art of
language. Yet to grasp the full meaning of the language
without imagining the unheard music conceived to accompany it would be next to impossible. Music is there,
all the more intense for being in so high and pure a regis-
ter that it transcends the literal ear.

"Ploughing on Sunday" is an artful verse-trifle in the

strong dipodic measures of popular balladry and children's songs. There is something to hear in each of its five short stanzas, as the rustle of feathers, the bluster of wind, or the resonance of rushing water. The poem fairly glitters with sound. The key itself is set by Remus, who blows his horn. In the third stanza Stevens employs one of his most typical and idiosyncratic devices, nonsense words, or rather, syllables, that nevertheless, like music, convey a meaning without language properly so called. Here it may be the strumming of a banjo: "Tum-ti-tum, ti-tum-tum-tum." Even in the instance of such humble nonsense one may speak of an apotheosis of poetry in the idiom of music. And it deserves notice that Stevens, ever an artist but never a snob, delights not only in the most delicate tones of harpsichord and clavier but in the simplest and most sensuous music of folk tune and folk instruments. Second only to the piano in his affection is the guitar, to which profuse reference is made in his poems. The poet of the blue guitar is seldom if ever removed from music, or, to express the matter differently, he is so only in the relatively minor number of his clearly inferior works, where the pursuit of pure reason temporarily alienates him from his true and better genius.

The structure of many of his finest poems clearly owes as much to musical as to literary form. In certain of his witty poems we keep hearing the brisk phrases and rhythms of the guitar; in his most rhetorical and baroque manner we hear the resonance of a baroque organ. Passing from style to composition, one observes his repeated attention to the formulas of theme and variation. In his earlier poems this device appears in its simplest and most elementary patterns, as in "Thirteen Ways of Looking at a Blackbird." In his later works he cultivates what may be described as elaborate fugal constructions, where, for example, a poem is in two parts, form in one meticulously mirroring that in the other. These variations give much pleasure and will actually repay far more attention than space permits here. But at least a brief description may be welcome.

"Thirteen Ways of Looking at a Blackbird" is one of the most highly perfected of Stevens' works. Its art has, perhaps, been more obscured than illumined by its popularity. Virtually from its first publication it has received considerable notoriety as a *tour de force*. The general reading public seems to have been more fascinated than seriously impressed, as though neither they nor its author should rightly take it seriously. The contrary is, of course, true. From one point of view it is, to be sure, a virtuoso study in imagery. Only two of the thirteen minute segments constituting the poem refer explicitly to sound. The whole stands in an unmistakable relation to the poetry of the Imagists and to the pictorial Japanese haiku. Yet the work might with almost equal propriety have been called, "Thirteen Ways of Hearing a Blackbird." For it is explicitly cast in the manner of theme and variations. Presumably it constitutes Stevens' happiest experiment in this type of composition, though several other of his pieces in various ways approximate it. Thus "Variations on a Summer Day" announces a similar technique in its title but offers a considerably looser approximation to the rigorous development of a musical idea. The individual items are strung upon a looser thread. And the fairly long "Like Decorations in a Nigger Cemetery" has little continuity, being for the most part merely a gathering of unrelated epigrams.

The musical overtone in Stevens' more successful poem is intimated in its movement from silence through sound to silence again. Numbers one and thirteen, the first and last sections, employ a wintry imagery in which the bird is imagined as austerely silent. Numbers five and ten stress the bird's call, lifting the poem to its more lyrical heights. In particular, section five, weighing the relative charms of the inflections and the innuendoes in the bird's call, shows how delicately Stevens' ear is tuned to essentially musical values. Music is as much in the background of the blackbird as in the background of that outstanding effusion, "Peter Quince at the Clavier," a poem to be examined later.

The strict pattern of theme and variation exhibited in his studies of the blackbird proved too elementary for him as his art matured. The parallelism represented by the art of the fugue better served his later purposes. The development is traceable in a comparison between "Certain Phenomena of Sound" and "Two Versions of the Same Poem." The first, a work of great delicacy, studies three varieties in significant sound through the medium of three related short poems merged into one. The sounds are alike in being all overtones, all accompaniments to certain actions, and all sounds less heard than overheard or even spectral. In the first instance old John Rocket breathes heavily and dozes to the reminiscent murmur of locusts' wings. Otherwise, the house is as empty as a bubble, as quiet as the silence of the industrious spider. All its slender meaning focuses on the locusts' wings. In the second section the sound of "a slick sonata" drifts through the doors and windows of a house to a garden where a lusty, arrogant adventurer relates to his family or friends the story of his recent travels. In the third section patients in a hospital weigh the dark sound of the name "Semiramide" with the white tone of the nurse's name, "Eulalia," each name describing the character of its owner. The essential meaning has mysteriously attached itself to the imaginative value of the personal names. The triptych in turn proceeds through quietude, lustiness, and mystery. It is not so much that a single theme has been varied as that a pattern has been followed out in three parallel forms. This tripartite work stands in a transitional position between "Thirteen Ways of Looking at a Blackbird" and "Two Versions of the Same Poem."

From fairly early in Stevens' career one poem tended to beget another more or less in its own image, only to yield its richest fruits under his most fully trained and long experienced hand. In his *Ideas of Order* (1936), for example, appear "Botanist on Alp (No. 1)" and "Botanist on Alp (No. 2)." *The Man with the Blue Guitar* (1937) contained "A Thought Revolved," a striking poem in four closely related but virtually self-sufficient parts. *Parts of a World* (1942) presents "Contrary Theses (1)," and "Contrary Theses (2)." In *Transport to Summer* (1947) we read "Two Tales of Liadoff." In *The Auroras of Autumn* (1950) we encounter "Study of Images I," and "Study of Images II." Finally, in his last volume, *The Rock*, are two unusually fine poems, "Two Illustrations That the World Is What You Make It." In these cases we are reminded less of parallel panels, a diptych or a triptych, than of musical constructions. As previously noted, perhaps the best example of this technique is "Two Versions of the Same Poem." In each version the basic idea is the dark, inveterate tendency of an encompassing force to weaken itself by subdivision.

The philosopher of the first section discovers a mysterious force within the ocean restlessly dividing itself into streams, currents, waves, meaningless expenditures of energy. The philosopher of the second section is old John Zeller, understood as a Christian pietist, who studies the cosmic upheavals with a similar despondency. He finds humanity, or perhaps better, modern humanity, an ocean beating itself helplessly against the rock of its fate. On deeper examination he even discovers the universe itself lacking in essential unity, for it is an oceanic concatenation of different elements, as water, earth, air, fire, all decomposing, like wave following wave, without purpose. He imagines their forms as vainly "seeking to escape cadaverous undulations." His final cry, a variation on words in *Hamlet*, is "rest, old Mould." This parallels the final exclamation of the first section: "Sleep deep, good eel, in your perverse marine." The parallelism of these final lines shows that Stevens' sense of abstract form, with obvious affinity to music, weighs more with him than variation upon any image, of either a strictly literary or a pictorial nature. The sections are, in fact, roughly paralleled throughout.

This intricate, highly self-conscious design in much of Stevens' poetry often comes closer to its sister art of music than to the pictorial arts with which he was also fruitfully familiar. "The Hermitage at the Center," in his last volume, *The Rock*, affords further striking illustration. This poem of fifteen lines is printed in five tercets. The first lines of these tercets, which are set off from the rest by dashes, constitute a complete sentence and well-rounded statement of an idea. The five pairs of slightly shorter lines in their turn make a logically sufficient statement. The poem would seem not only to be two poems forcibly joined as one but to be a dialogue of two persons at first deliberately speaking at cross purposes. Yet the real point, revealed in the actual conclusion, draws the two opposed elements together. One statement insists that life is transient and tottering, the other that it is a rich experience varied to the degree of the unintelligible. In the end, natural intuition, or art relying on the sensuous world, finds even a rational resolution of an only apparent contradiction. The two opposing voices are at last harmonized. The images, in short, remain disparate until the end, when a formal mastery akin to music draws the disjointed members together. It would be difficult indeed to read this poem without awareness of its analogy to music. We have a lyric in the madrigal manner.

In the achievement of Stevens' success in an essentially lyrical style, his approximation to dance forms proves almost as conspicuous as that to music. Although an intensely meditative man, he is deeply in love with motion, and motion strongly physical and homocentric. His position here stands close to the religious and poetic mind of India. Without overindulging his inclination for allegory or for mythological symbolism, he shows a liking for the conception even of natural forms as moving in dance-like patterns. Thus one of his finest poems, "Domination of Black," becomes a dance pantomime of flying sparks, wind-swept leaves, the wind-blown tails of peacocks, the swaying branches of the hemlocks, and even the motion of the stars. The universe itself seems whirling away in a mysterious, sinister, wind-blown dance motion, the movement of some impassioned maenad.

The first poem of his first volume, "Earthy Anecdote," represents a savage dance in nature, a pantomime of the mindless, spacious American West, where on the open plain in Oklahoma the bucks and the firecat enact their wild gyrations. Both this poem and "Domination of Black" have other and probably more important values than their affinity to a sense for the dance and will accordingly be considered in other contexts. The same applies to the second of Stevens' plays, "Carlos among the Candles," which is essentially a dance poem or at least one in which dance-pantomime carries as much weight as the words themselves. The simplest instance is "Life Is Motion," a little poem of twenty-one words, with the assistance of two cries not to be found in any dictionary. The lines describe the dancing around a stump by Bonnie and Josie, who in this primitive fashion celebrate "the marriage of flesh and air." Their dance is described as taking place in Oklahoma, thus suggesting to Stevens' reader his lines on the bucks and the firecat, celebrating a scene in the same locality. Primitive dancing becomes an important theme in two of his most sustained poems, "Sunday Morning" and "Esthétique du Mal." Much of his best work throbs with the feeling of the dance. A lyric strength quite obvious in *Harmonium* but even more deeply implanted in some of the finest of his later poetry clearly owes much to a sensibility in step with the movement of dancers. A few of his poems have, in fact, been used as inspiration for choreography, as by one of his fellow citizens of Hartford, Ruth Grauert, now of the notable Henry Street Dance Group, New York.

No concentration upon philosophical aesthetics prevented Stevens from excelling in a considerable variety of well-known poetic forms. His ideas tend to proliferate from a single stem, whereas his forms multiply freely as his explorative genius guides him. One field assiduously cultivated is the verse epigram, or very short poem. His editor, Samuel French Morse, observes that such a manner is apparent not merely in his briefest poems but pervasively in all his work, rich in succinct, quotable aphorism, after the manner of Pope and the Augustans. Yet his usual style is by no means prickly or short-winded, merely witty with the quest for epigram, as in Oscar Wilde's prose, and some distinction, though not a rigid one, should be made between his short, imagistic poems, roughly in the Japanese manner, and his terse satirical epigrams close to the classical tradition. Thus the thirteen short impressionistic poems constituting "Thirteen Ways of Looking at a Blackbird" contrast with the rhymed, witty couplets of "New England Verses," which better than any of his other pieces show his skill in the traditional epigram, though this is in its execution one of the most original of his strictly patterned pieces.

"New England Verses" are only in part about New England, although they exhibit New England's familiar tendencies toward transcendentalism in philosophy, class-consciousness in manners, and internationalism in general orientation. More important, at least for the present argument, is the self-conscious style, the extreme economy of statement, and the pointed wit which reserves its sting for the last word or two of the statements. The couplets are arranged in pairs, the second couplet in each pair presenting the antithesis of the first. Furthermore, the same formula is used in the witty titles provided for all the couplets, the titles themselves arranged in pairs. This is highly intellectual verse, rendered poetic and even elusive largely because of the imaginative imagery and breadth of thought in counterpoint with its succinctness of expression. Penetrating comments occur in turn on such paradoxical problems as the outlook that renders each individual the center of the universe or excludes him from participation in the objective universe; on the collision of democratic and aristocratic theories; on pedantry versus sensuality, the former in overt league with idealism; on social consciousness as opposed to retirement of the individual; on the proud, self-sufficient individual and the inglorious and formless crowd; on intellectual and aesthetic elegance as opposed to deliberate barbarism; on inveterate cynicism and sophisticated sensuality; on decadence and a fresh perfection. These attitudes are all pertinent to New England thought, with its strongly accented ironies and contradictions. Each couplet is powerfully imaginative and clearly poetic at the same time that it constitutes a blow in behalf of trenchant social and aesthetic criticism. The couplets, too profound for currency in popular quotation, are sparks of a strongly original mind.

His poetry ranges from some of the weightiest to some of the lightest types of verse. The pervasive irony and general sophistication of his style have apparently concealed other no less important features from many of his critics, who prefer to describe him as a difficult poet and remain unwilling to acknowledge either the moral and emotional seriousness of certain of his poems or the lightness and grace of others. His poems always reveal a highly conscientious workmanship but otherwise move in several widely divergent directions. Such a philosophical elegy as "Esthétique du Mal" is eminently serious. But what shall be said of comic trifles like "Table Talk"? Here the title faithfully indicates the unquestionable levity of style. It is in Stevens' most colloquial and least rhetorical manner. Since no baroque rhetoric similar to that of "Le Monocle de Mon Oncle" occurs, he cannot even smile at his own flourishes. Such a work is frankly light verse of a high quality, graceful, urbane, and little more, even though its subject, the relativity of truth, is developed elsewhere by Stevens with high seriousness. In this instance he handles his theme with his very lightest touch. Sound art results, but not art in one of its highest categories. It may be significant that although the piece was written when he was well advanced in his career, approximately 1935, a man approaching sixty, he did not see fit to publish it in any of his volumes. It was printed in that sprightly avant-garde little magazine *Rocking Horse*. Yet this, too, is a significant part of Stevens' story. He can neither be summarily described as the Crispin, or Harlequin, that he frequently claims to be, nor as the ponderous rabbi that he also claims to be and that he is more often said to be by his critics. The Stevens of a considerable number of witty and charming trivia may be included among our foremost masters of light verse.

The considerable range of his tone appears when such a graceful trifle as "Table Talk" is contrasted with such a piece of unquestionably satirical verse as "A High-Toned Old Christian Woman." This extremely well-written poem aims not only to delight its reader but to "make widows wince." Self-satire does not produce the pure type of literary satire. Hence "Le Monocle de Mon Oncle," or much of "The Comedian as the Letter C," does not fall into the category most justly or commonly regarded as satire. But "A High-Toned Old Christian Woman," with its Shavian bite, is specifically satire, for the imagined speaker places himself in a flattering light and his victim in an absurd one. An attack, even though risible, is apparent. Amused or possibly offended by the narrow pretentiousness of a conventional moralist, a widow of monstrous virtue, the poet reminds her that her projection of a heaven of virtue on earth holds no more ultimate validity than a poet's hedonistic projection of a heaven of ultimate delight. In his best rhetorical manner Stevens ridicules a pretentious asceticism which to the impartial mind must seem fantastically ludicrous. Since a large part of Stevens' poetry is either self-satire or a broad ironic smiling at our possibly pathetic human condition, this example of his rarer tendency to frank attack stands out prominently.

Savage indignation he seldom admits, yet he often maintains a serious and an indisputably moral view of human affairs. He seems to have been embarrassed by his own descent to satire. So in the monumental volume *Collected Poems*, issued in his seventy-fifth year, he permitted the omission of one of his best-written pieces, "Owl's Clover," with its occasional contemporary allusions, and his own comments diminished the value of his few lesser pieces with direct satirical reference, as the witty "Lytton Strachey, Also, Enters into Heaven," reminiscent of Vachel Lindsay's poem on General William Booth. His personal temperament was almost over-retiring. He disliked the heated controversy of the market place. Consequently, his readers are quite likely to discover more merit in his satirical passages than he himself was disposed to admit. His hatred of war, for example, called forth some violent comments and he was the author of a few of the most savage and withering lines in American poetry. Of this elsewhere. Here it suffices to establish the existence of at least a few straightforward satirical poems.

Satire suggests comment on men in action and hence comment in a dramatic vein. Stevens' breadth appears in nothing more strikingly than in his occasional inclination toward the dramatic mood and form. Drama exists in the artistic perfection of conflict, climax, and surprise, in the presentation of life heightened with tension and excitement. It need not be verbal but it must be sharp, tense, suspended along the coordinates of time. It must also be physical, for acting is organized gesture, as dancing is organized bodily movement. Drama is even more occupied with tension and climax than the dance, and similarly, being less abstract, adds expression of the face to expression of the body. It would be a grave error to presume that the essential idea of the dramatic is confined to theatrical literature or performance. Clouds move dramatically. The sun and moon are greatest of dramatists. Music, painting, architecture, and especially sculpture can be strongly dramatic. Even the short poem has been host to highly dramatic expression. It is possible that Emily Dickinson at no time witnessed a stage play, but in her poetry she dramatized her own life and the lives of her friends with astonishing force. The opposite of the dramatic may appear as the contemplative, and Stevens is first of all a contemplative man. Yet out of religious contemplation springs much of the unsurpassed Sanskrit drama. It may even be urged that at least some ingredient of the dramatic is essential for any successful artistic creation.

Although the general bias of his thought and temper discouraged Stevens from dramatic writing in either the more abstract or the more literal sense of the word, he was too broad-minded and virile an artist to forgo either the vigor of dramatic effect in his customary poems or even the attraction of a minimum of theatrical writing. Happily, the dramatic force and form held some charm for him and must be added to the appraisal of his gifts in philosophical poetry, the lyric, epigram, and satire.

Drama's sword is absolute and conclusive. It carves not only in terms of climax but in terms of entrances and exits, the beginning and the end. Any number of Stevens' poems have sharp, theatrical beginnings, as an inspection of their first lines conspicuously shows. But the abrupt and surprising conclusion usually gives still more striking evidence of the dramatic. A considerable number of his poems provide really alarming endings. Stevens well knows the value of the stark, resonant chord, so modern and so distinct from the peaceable ending in the classical tradition. This shows most conspicuously in leisurely, reflective, philosophical pieces rising to sharp action in their final phrases. So in "Extracts from Addresses to the Academy of Fine Ideas" he proceeds from one meditation to another with the profound, leisurely, almost imperceptible motion of the summer clouds which he loves. With the last page he speculates on the job of achieving just one line or phrase whose music, image, thought will be wholly adequate. The entire

poem, then, comes to its conclusion with two lines, related
to the whole merely as an instance of what the poet offers
as a product of the imagination as nearly as possible perfect. The theme proves most appropriate for an idealistic
poet in the twentieth century: a profound hatred of war
and its military standards of value:

> Behold the men in helmets borne on steel
> Discolored, how they are going to defeat.

A reflective poem ends with a gesture of intensely dramatic
feeling.

More striking and more typical is an instance in a more
strictly ordered poem, "The Bouquet," appearing in a
volume a few years later. "The Bouquet" is a metaphysical
and philosophical poem on Stevens' favorite theme,
aesthetic imagination as the most gratifying means of
encompassing reality. The secondary and the primary
meanings of the flowers composing the bouquet are
studied in a poem as searching as the most inspired of still-
life paintings. Only the mind moves. The physical world is
arrested by the bouquet, whose inner movements and significations the poet restlessly explores. Thus far the poem
is sedulously undramatic. But Stevens provides an ending
almost as theatrical as in the best of Chekhov or O'Casey.

The body of the poem is a *tour de force* in contemplation. It is worth notice, to begin with, that the profuse
imagery associated with the bouquet abounds in surprises
in themselves sharply dramatic, even though the still-life
theme stands in sharp contrast with the dramatic. This is
actually one of the conspicuous dramatic formulas of
Stevens' verse. Earlier poems may be cited. "The Glass of
Water" likens the sunlight in the glass to a lion come

down to drink. "Woman Looking at a Vase of Flowers" begins with a description of the violent colors of the flowers as thunder taking form upon the piano. The reader need not know Stevens' fairly elaborate though by no means pedantic personal symbolism of color to appreciate the extreme dramatic tensions lying deep within the poet's imagination contemplating the bouquet in the poem here chiefly considered. The flowers, the vase, the table-cloth are outwardly motionless but to the imagination activated with tempestuous life. Especially indicative surprises occur, as in the last line of the second section, where the thought of "a woman standing in such a dress" abruptly obtrudes. The contrasted white and red squares of the table-cloth blend into a single tone; there is drama in the fallen petals, as in those still clinging precariously to their flowers. Violent action and the most static form are held in suspense or equilibrium, which is itself a species of theatrical repose.

Then, without the slightest warning, the major surprise occurs. We see the bouquet through the strictly theatrical eye, the outer eye that perceives significant motion in the physical world. After vainly ringing and knocking, a soldier enters the empty room. As he hurries past on his sinister mission, he hits the table and the bouquet falls on its side. After searching the house, he returns and hurriedly exits, unconsciously knocking the vase to the floor. This violent action contrasts the profound inner imaginings and sensitivity of the poetic mind with the notorious callousness of the military mind. A singularly contemplative poem comes to a vigorously theatrical conclusion.

The body of the foregoing poem suggests, as Stevens himself confessed, that he was overmuch concerned with

things and too little occupied with people. Stevens is victim of place and thing. This further implies that he has
relatively small contact with narratives. Most of his longest poems, as "Esthétique du Mal," "An Ordinary Evening in New Haven," "The Man with the Blue Guitar,"
"Notes toward a Supreme Fiction," or "Examination of
the Hero in a Time of War" conspicuously dispense with
narrative, and his shorter poems have in general little or
no relation with balladry or other types of narrative verse.
But again there are exceptions. Here are, under the circumstances, rather surprising signs of breadth, suggesting
a revision of any facile categorizing. He wrote several dramatic monologues. Only an unsophisticated reader will
overlook the frequent presence of either autobiographical
statement or full objectivity. The uncle of the celebrated
poem on middle age comes at least closer to being a dramatic character than to being the poet, though certainly
the poet felt, as all persons must, some potential kinship
with the aging man who talks to cheer himself up. Stevens
dramatically disguises himself as Peter Quince and other
imaginary figures. Clearly, he is and he is not the Crispin
of "The Comedian as the Letter C," one of his longest and
most ambitious works. The baroque manner which he so
much affects is itself highly dramatic. A few poems in
dialogue occur, as "The Plot against the Giant," whose
three stanzas are successively spoken by three girls.

Most surprising in this connection is a bold excursion
into semi-narrative, "Page from a Tale," whose title proves
fairly descriptive. Only a very discerning reader, impressed
by its quiet irony, would imagine it to be by Wallace
Stevens. The irony lies in the whimsical quotations from
William Butler Yeats's celebrated and romantic lyric

"The Lake Isle of Innisfree." In his own composition Stevens aims at expressing the position of the complete realist. Isolation is in his eyes no blessing. He imagines a steamer shipwrecked off an Arctic coast. Those aboard prefer the risk of crossing by night the rough ice lying between them and the deserted shore to waiting for daylight, when the sun may melt or disperse the ice and so keep them forever from land. "Page from a Tale" is a rude bit of savage drama somewhat in the manner of a sensational popular film or even of such a melodrama as the famous play drawn from *Uncle Tom's Cabin*. Typical of Stevens' speculations is the distinction between the mindless, monotonous roar of the waves, sounds as barren of meaning and grossly romantic as Yeats's poem, and the inflections of the wind, now soft, now loud, whose almost articulate tones are emulated in Stevens' realism. This refinement of thought appears at both the beginning and end of the poem. The rest, except for the brief intrusions of ironic quotation from Yeats, remains fairly straightforward melodramatic narrative.

Incipient drama occurs in an early poem, written about 1920, "Infernale." This is a slightly ribald dialogue between a rude inhabitant of "middle earth" and Persephone, as she ascends on her annual visit to earth and to Olympus, the wax that sealed her fast in hell melted away. Stevens never included the poem in any of his volumes and, as far as I am aware, it first saw publication in *Opus Posthumous*. Before writing this striking scene of drama in miniature he had written his two notable plays, his poetic play roughly in the manner of the pseudo-Noh drama, "Three Travelers Watch a Sunrise," and the dance monodrama, "Carlos among the Candles," both published, with honors, in *Poetry*. Inasmuch as Stevens remarked that he sent his best pieces to that magazine, we have further evidence that both should be taken more seriously than they have been by most of his commentators.

Like the rest of Stevens' work, these bold experiments in dramatic form appeal both to the senses and to the mind; they are, in other words, both spectacles and philosophical disquisitions. Each contains much pantomime and strong emphasis on the play of light. "Carlos among the Candles" has dance movement throughout. Each begins in darkness and is thereafter illumined by candlelight. In one the light gradually increases, with a sunrise rich in color at its conclusion. The other glitters at its midpoint with twenty-four candles, returning in the end to the darkness with which it began. In both cases the literary style is for Stevens comparatively unadorned, the words lightly sketched on the surface of the action but of great delicacy. Save for one brief song, "Three Travelers Watch a Sunrise" is presented as free verse, with very short lines. Although "Carlos among the Candles" is printed as prose, its rhythms actually are more pronounced than those of the earlier play and it is indubitably poetic. Stevens' work here is possibly best described, after the fashion set by Baudelaire, as a prose poem.

Each play deals with problems in aesthetics, the first largely with questions of reality and the expression of emotion, the second with both the emotions and the stylistic effects regarded as most appropriate for poetry. Although both bear some likeness to Yeats's "dance dramas," inspired by that poet's study of Japanese Noh plays, neither of Stevens' works appears closely to resemble anything else in dramatic literature in any tongue. The Oriental characters in the earlier play, taken together with the approximations to Oriental thought and style suggest his acquaintance with the drama of the Far East in some form. The approximation to Yeats is less likely to have been weighed as a consideration of importance. The temper of both plays, rich in symbolism, in aesthetic speculation, and in severe concentration, accords with prevailing tendencies throughout Stevens' poetry. The plays are his. They might be almost infinitely suggestive to playwrights working in poetic drama, but little or no evidence exists that the world of the stage considered them seriously and still less that since their publication they have received the attention as literature which they so obviously deserve. They are highly original works of great force and beauty.

"Three Travelers Watch a Sunrise" stages a debate between three Chinese sages, the first and third advocating a wholly unimpassioned view of life, a view primarily occupied with conceptions of decorative form, the second offering an apology for emotion in art and for a man's living with frank recognition of evil, ugliness, and privation. The two represent a courtly doctrine, the single voice, a plea for the more humane art which Stevens himself clearly favors. These choral figures, in turn a hedonist, a humanist, and an aesthete, occupy the center of the stage and so far as there is any real action they perform it. But in the usual theatrical sense there is no action. The advent of day reveals a corpse hanging from a tree. A weeping girl gradually becomes visible. In a bare score of lines she relates the fantastic story that she and the man whose body hangs on the tree walked together to the hilltop which provides the scene of the action and that there her lover hung himself. The sages reflect on the relativity of pain, which is diversified among observers of a single incident, as the experience of the sunrise and all experiences of art are subject to relativity. Relativity is human; precision is merely mechanistic. The most remarkable feature of this profoundly symbolical play is the play-within-the-play, two narratives resembling ballads presented by the sages and projected in imagery on the water jar placed in the center of the stage. By carefully worked-out analogies, the jar is the world, its figures are the ballad characters, and the candle held beside it is the sun. The jar thus introduces the characters whose story later becomes the theme presented in the play as real life. Thus Stevens gains carefully arranged levels or strata of dramatic intensity. It should be added that much of the play is ornamented with music, giving it as a whole the quality of music drama.

Although no mention is made of music in "Carlos among the Candles," the pervasive dance movement makes music virtually essential. A fantastic, old-fashioned gentleman of forty enters a room with a lighted taper. On seeing tables ornamented with candles, he proceeds to light them one by one, speaking a monologue as he does so. One candle suggests to him loneliness; two suggest respectable companionship; three, elegance; four, the beginning of luxury; five, magnificence; six, splendor; seven, a city. When he has lit twenty-four, he commences to extinguish them, with similar comments. In the end, feeling that the lights have merely illuminated illusion, he leaps through a window into an outer darkness bearing an ironic promise of reality. Though defying most of the precepts placed before the playwright of the Western world, both plays are profoundly dramatic, with a fine sense for theatrical gesture and design.

IV : *Phases of Style*

BROADLY speaking, Stevens' poetry is the contemplation of a basic theme, the aesthetic imagination. Sometimes he writes of human imagination in general but it is clear that he has small interest in the imagination in science, in the political world, or in other major areas of speculation. His mind operates forcefully within the area commonly considered the humanities; his acknowledged unwillingness to come to grips with other provinces, notably those of current public affairs, indicates the boundaries encircling his none-the-less wide domain. His position should be viewed in the light of comparative literature. To Dante as poet, for example, virtually all known areas of thought were accessible. Undeniably, in comparison with Dante, Stevens' thought seems specialized and confined. But so does the thought of by far the greater number of the world's poets and Stevens is no more limited in this regard than the average illustrious name. His sharply distinguished position lies less in the degree of his limitations than in their conspicuousness. It is, to repeat, as obvious that he is a poet of the philosophy of aesthetics as that Lucretius is a poet of the philosophy of nature. Both use their insights as contributions to the enrichment of human living. Both are luminous poets, neither falling for more than a few passages into the aridities of a no man's land between poetry on the one hand and philosophical speculation on the other.

Stevens' area of poetic discourse proves even more restricted than has been indicated thus far. His mind dwells on extremes of the particular and the abstract. His failure to write thoroughly successful drama and his total neglect of prose fiction or even of a fully developed narrative poetry spring in part from his neglect of the personal view of life. Success in drama or narrative is denied him primarily because his thought either on the physical world, with the sensations and ideas which it arouses, or on general and abstract ideas proceeds with relatively little cognizance of the wide intervening area. Although his philosophy scrupulously respects the human individuality, it shows scant interest in exploring the mysteries of individuality or, in other words, the outlines of personality in life or characterization in art. Life without human freedom this New England poet regards as misery, but he easily dispenses with explorations into the characters of real or imaginary individuals. For such explorations there is good reason to suppose that he holds the highest respect; but these are simply not his own concerns as poet and artist. It is not that he denies their validity. In fact, his own theoretical speculations clear a broad, smooth highway in their direction. But on the way he finds so much rich land to cultivate that he remains content with his own elected province.

If Stevens conspicuously lacks the feminine sense for

personality and that refinement of gossip which we commonly call fiction, to an exceptional degree he possesses a feminine sense for place and physical environment and for the spiritual values of the most minor obects in the physical world. On the one hand, he is a poetical geographer or landscape painter; on the other, a scholar of minutiae and a still-life painter. This peculiar orientation he established early in his career as poet and maintained to the last. It is clear that he writes in the age of the modern camera, which illuminates both these extremes—though the Far East has for centuries been familiar with the dual focus. His "Comedian as the Letter C" is essentially no more than its definition. Stevens became the sure appraiser of the cultural significance of climatic distinctions, the spiritual meanings of tropical and northern climes, the connoisseur of atmosphere, surpassing in this regard even Monet, for the clear reason that he explored fully not only the distinctions of the four seasons within the temperate zone but significant distinctions of land and sky from Maine to Florida or from the sub-tropics to the sub-Arctic. For him, as "The Comedian as the Letter C" and "Farewell to Florida" so clearly show, the tropics signify a lush, rhetorical manner, the northern countries a stark austerity of style.

This gift for imagining the physical world in large, sweeping terms naturally accompanied a gift for the historical imagination, the imagination which Stevens reveals so remarkably in "Owl's Clover," a work which in this connection may be regarded as the companion piece to "The Comedian as the Letter C." Stevens himself was almost embarrassed by the warmth of his own historical imagination, as it brought him into impassioned contact even with the largest accumulations of men. His historical imagination glows with a disturbing heat possibly even greater than his warmth in the more narrow and explicitly personal aspects of life. Viewing the social disasters of the twentieth century and roughly similar disasters of earlier times, he experienced emotional alarm. He shuddered. "Owl's Clover" was expurgated from his *Collected Poems*.

On the other extreme Stevens, whose imaginary projection is the Crispin of his first long poem, becomes a miniaturist, "the lutanist of fleas," the high priest celebrating the minute perfections of melons, peaches, and pears. In other words, he has the eye of Chardin as well as of Ruysdael. All this is, in fact, a modern projection or exaggeration of attitudes typically baroque. Following Pascal and Bossuet, he reaches toward the sublime and the grand, venturing even to the verge of the grandiose; following such artists as Vermeer and Watteau, or the twentieth-century cult of still-life painters, he ventures to the verge of the absurdly finicky, precious, and over-refined. As a poetical painter of nature he can rival Milton in sublimity or James Thomson, author of *The Seasons*, in attention to what William Blake termed "minute particulars."

Stevens, in short, saw life through a series of lenses, some telescopic, some microscopic, but he seldom perceived it through the normal naked eye. Nevertheless, he had far more than two optical adjustments at his disposal. Rooms he seldom describes; the décor of interiors he leaves largely to novelists and realistic stage designers, who stand in danger of forsaking the poet's ideal occupation with universality. Accordingly, laborious descriptions of interiors, or, for that matter, of exteriors, he scrupulously shuns. But as he himself said, his mind naturally focuses upon place, which is to say, upon landscapes, seascapes, vistas, parks, public squares, and urban outlooks in general. In these areas he is most at home.

His extraordinarily penetrating views of the seasons of the year aid rather than limit his sense for place, since in appreciating the seasons either descriptively or symbolically some location or point of view is eminently useful. It is scarcely necessary in this connection to recall the titles of two of his books, *Transport to Summer* and *The Auroras of Autumn*, or to note that his first volume, *Harmonium*, is refreshed with generous images of spring —"The Paltry Nude Starts on a Spring Voyage"—and that his *Opus Posthumous* contains several especially memorable poems on winter, written during the last years of his life, as "On the Way to the Bus." The poet conveys an imaginative meaning for winter by evoking a specific scene in that season, not by comments of a general nature. In this regard he proceeds from the particular to the general. He leads us to a definite, wintry place before arriving at his imaginative interpretation of winter.

This symbolical awareness of place appears throughout his work, from the poem chosen to be first in his first volume to what is obviously one of the outstanding poems in the last collection published in his own lifetime, "To an Old Philosopher in Rome." "Earthy Anecdote," on the first page of *Harmonium*, is a robust bit of Americana, like music by Stevens' neighbor, Charles Ives, or painting by his contemporary, Marsden Hartley, or "Appalachian Spring," most ingratiating of the dances created by still another American master in modern art, Martha Graham.

This unassuming little masterpiece has its scene in one of the most provincial of the American states, Oklahoma. It depicts animal movements strikingly like those of the dance: the ballet of pursuit and escape enacted by a wildcat and a group of young horses. The subject of the poem, stated more explicitly in the already-examined piece, "Life Is Motion," is the exhilarating union of motion, light, and air, the sense of the freedom of space and the ecstasy of free movement within it. Although the avowed subject is physical, the significance extends also to the mental and the spiritual. Whatever sordidness the social scene in Oklahoma may possess is overlooked in view of the vivid realization of it very literally as land of the free and home of the brave. Its implications notwithstanding, the poem is basically optimistic and naïve. Stevens' own term for such thinking is "archaic" or "antique." Both the word "antique" and the idea are contained in a later and decidedly sophisticated poem, also dealing with horses, "Parochial Theme," significantly chosen as the first poem in *Parts of a World*. This initial evocation of place symbolizes the basic healthy, physical impulses of life; man as attuned to nature in a state of moral innocence simply because morality does not exist within these primitive terms.

Of course not all the poems in *Harmonium* are in the area of thought and expression so well represented by "Earthy Anecdote." Yet it remains distinctly meaningful that several poems in much the same spirit are found there and that, in fact, throughout his entire life as poet Stevens is capable of entertaining its thought and feeling and of writing in this straightforward manner. But for the present argument the chief consideration is the infatuation with place. Here it is the least complicated place. "To an Old Philosopher in Rome," probably the finest poem in his final volume, *The Rock*, still clings to place, although in this later instance the place is one of the most time-burdened, historical, and supersophisticated cities in the Western world. Surely the contrast is eloquent and yet the likeness proves even more so. From first to last from the imaginative point of view place governs the poem. That these conditions exist is obvious even at a glance. Yet some effort is required to construe the many refinements in the later work and at least some further account of it in terms of the present argument is desirable.

Actually the character described is George Santayana, but this philosopher, essayist, and poet is not named nor is it desirable that he should be. Imagination, Stevens holds, demands abstraction. There is really no appraisal of Santayana as a thinker beyond the implication that he stands in a great tradition. Stevens does not even make clear his own estimate of such conservatism, and in view of his own strong inclinations to experimentation and modernity, and of his love for Oklahoma, good reason exists to believe that Stevens honors the great traditionalist without following consistently in his footsteps. The pith of the poem is its penetration into the relation of person and place, and the place is shown as dominating the person rather than the person the place. The philosopher in this instance complies with his environment and becomes its spokesman. The Roman way is for him a good and sufficient way. The city, both in its physical and social coloration and in its religious, political, and philosophical implications, is enough. The aged man, even near to death, accepts what his city, its folkways and its philosophical highways, have given him. He lives and dies a part of his place, of his environment, the quintessence of his inherited Mediterranean tradition. The poem is one of resignation made beautiful because the soul resigns itself to such humane and such noble causes.

It should be especially noted that place is here more important and more inclusive than any religious institution or philosophical system for which it supplies the frame. To describe this aged man as dying in the arms of the Church or of the old philosophers would grotesquely misrepresent the case. His life and death represent a total immersion in the life and soul of a real and yet symbolic city. The gentle murmurs of the nuns, the crude babble of sounds filtering from the streets, are as much a vital part of the conception, even a more vital part, as any dogma whatsoever, theological, philosophical, or political. It is as much from the ignominy as from the grandeur of Rome that its sublimity arises. Stevens' imagination, which in his earliest poems rose to the very serious challenge of Oklahoma, ascended at last to the much more arduous challenge of Rome. The later poem is doubtless the finer as it certainly is the more artful or complex, but both are good; each is virtually perfect in its own kind; and each supplies evidence of the poet's imaginative grasp of locality. The first poem has something of the purity of Scottish song or German Lieder; the second vies with Yeats's most profound odes on the theme of the old age of the individual and the decadence of society. Place has been used, vastly enlarged, but not transcended, for it is upheld in spiritual and poetic apotheosis.

Searching the imaginative harvests of place and especially those of nature, Stevens' restive imagination often found flowing waters or floating clouds more fruitful than hard-surfaced land. Much the most brilliant of his descriptive pieces is "Sea Surface Full of Clouds." This is a set piece, less imaginative or profound than such later works as "Credences of Summer," "The Auroras of Autumn," or "Chocorua to Its Neighbor." Stevens' own allusion to a "pistache one," "good clown," "turquoise-turbaned Sambo," and the state of being "perfected in indolence," all in the final stanza, show that this monstrous and splendid feat of ingenuity and virtuosity even at the time of its writing was not taken by its author overseriously. Yet here is a marvelous jugglery of words in tribute to place— the tropical sea and sky in a united seascape. Stevens knew well that this poem had its roots in nineteenth-century Impressionism, not in strictly modern art from the advent of Picasso and later. The line of French verse quoted in each stanza reveals its pastiche and derivative quality. Stevens shows himself completely the master of lessons of French poetry from Baudelaire to Rimbaud, Valéry, Apollinaire, and Léon-Paul Fargue, as his sensibility made him the heir of Debussy, Milhaud, and Poulenc in music and Monet, Cézanne, and Picasso in painting. This poem uses all the stops on his baroque-rhetorical organ. The technique itself anchors the glowing scene in place. There are five eighteen-line stanzas consisting of six triplets. Their first lines are identical, the second lines all nearly so, but not quite the same, while the third line invariably ends with the word "deck," the fourth with "chocolate," the fifth with "green," and the sixth with "machine." The twelfth line is always in French. Each stanza presents the blue ocean under the threat of losing its serenity through assaults of wind and cloud, and in each case the threat is averted apparently by the incantation of a few French words. There are even sexual overtones to this seascape. One is reminded of Ovid's tale of Proteus and the sea nymph, or of Milhaud's witty rendering of it in music. The menace mounts to its climax in stanza four, where the threat of ravishment is once more thwarted so that its last appearance in stanza five can be construed only in a humorous spirit. What happens four times must be true.

This is an enchanted sea and sky, equally like nature and like magic. The smooth handling of bizarre images and the complete control of imagery and verse music become virtually miraculous. Words have seldom been polished to such a sparkling iridescence. Place has been dramatized into a baroque, amorous comedy of the elements, or the elements themselves utterly tamed and reduced to the suave urbanity of chocolate, porcelain, and gilt umbrellas. This will seem a sentimental world beyond good and evil, passion and pain, if it is not realized that calm has its validity no less than storm and that, to use Stevens' words, the hairy saints of the North have not—at least as yet— destroyed civilization. This celebration of place and of sensual pleasure should be handled lovingly and deposited on its shelf with other consummate masterpieces of the porcelain-maker's art. No other poem in English is quite like it. But certain elements which Stevens elsewhere richly supplies this work conspicuously lacks, as passion, thought, and simplicity.

"Sea Surface Full of Clouds" is pure Impressionism; it is also the apotheosis of rhetoric, glorious words lavishly deployed to no really serious purpose. Even when writing the piece, as its final stanza shows, Stevens was in no sense carried away by its cloudy, glistening speciousness, its celebration of the surface of things. The poem doubtless has its sophisticated allegory, its levels of meaning, as already indicated, but it remains sophisticated and lacking not only in profundity but in true modernity. This is, I believe, a much finer poem than any of the roughly analogous pieces by Swinburne, but it still reflects literary values now relatively out of fashion. It proves, in a word, too "poetic," using the term in its derogatory sense. Its style is ultrapoetic and basically sentimental, although the phenomenal self-consciousness, ingenuity, and wit in Stevens' technique save it from completely meretricious sentimentality. Its sentiment is an assumption, not a conviction—to use Stevens' terms, "ex-bar" and not "in-bar." But as he shrewdly remarked in his critique of his friend, William Carlos Williams, the sentimentalist is often thrown by reversal of forces into the antipoetic. Stevens never thought of himself as cultivating the antipoetic from this motive, for, quite rightly, he knew himself to be free from bourgeois sentimentality. Yet he knew acutely the insidious charms of the rhetoric so magnificently mastered in "Sea Surface Full of Clouds," as also in "Sunday Morning," and "To the One of Fictive Music." The latter poem is both a moving and an exquisite defense of a rich style, not as a parody of itself, as in "Le Monocle de Mon Oncle," but as a sincere vehicle for all the energy and resources of the imagination, as the poet's charter distinguishing him from the master of utilitarian prose.

To the end of his life Stevens was a poet-rhetorician, like Shakespeare and Milton. But he explored the dubious byways of virtuosity with a cool head and an uncommon discernment and unquestionably felt the seductions of virtuosity to an uncommon degree. Virtuosity was an evil mistress whom he knew well. Repeatedly he disciplines himself by reminders that imaginative truth rejects spurious rhetoric, that ornament which is inorganic is also inartful, and that Cézanne's naked trees are more moving and imaginative than Monet's trees fuzzy with their great weight of foliage. His good taste spurned the clichés of conventional and obsolete poetic diction. He demanded hard reality. The foliage of rhetoric might be encouraged but the roots of the tree itself were to be wedged between hard rock. The greatest elegance is the greatest simplicity.

Stevens was too aristocratic a man and too serenely contained an artist to squander words in teasing the public. Unlike the inhabitants of the left bank, he had no desire to shock the public, no matter how dull he conceived the public to be. He, too, remained in as many ways conservative as progressive. Slang had no attraction for him. Standard meters usually proved useful, though he dispensed as a rule with rhyme and cared relatively little for ready-made stanza forms. Actually, he is more a traditionalist than T. S. Eliot, who at least during one period of his career leaned upon American jazz and the London music halls. Stevens' deep fondness for imagery from nature associates him with the Georgians. But as a humorist he took too much pleasure in the naughtiness of real life to undervalue frank statements and harsh images accepted by the people and the avant-garde and renounced by the torpid bourgeoisie, or the American middle class. He composed at least one celebrated poem primarily to remind himself of his own perils as author in such lines as "Sea Surface Full of Clouds." This disturbing little work, "The Emperor of Ice Cream," written self-consciously and partly as an

act of penance, has often been taken more seriously than
its merits warrant. But it is undeniably amusing.

The poem so much resembles William Carlos Williams' delightfully mischievous "Tract," published a few
years earlier, that one wonders whether Stevens had his
friend's lines in the back of his mind when he wrote. Or
were they both merely taking the undertaker for a ride?
Each poem scandalously mocks the vacuous decorum of
modern funeral customs by imagining obsequies in an
ultraproletarian style. "Her bony feet protrude" in
Stevens' poem comes remarkably close to the spirit of Williams' antipoetic imagery. But Stevens' poem is gayer and
on the whole better. The "concupiscent curds" and the
general lustiness in Stevens' work have a conviction not
quite equaled by Williams' charming and colloquially expressed fantasy. Of the two poets, paradoxically enough,
the aristocratic, fastidious, and almost affected Stevens is
really the more robust and the lustier enjoyer of the world.
In brazen confidence he addresses death, which alone dissolves all things. To express this mood he invokes death
in the most demotic terms possible, as lord of that most
perishable of foods, ice cream. In his ironic role as champion of realism he enjoyed his innocent jest, whereas the
public, even when it did not understand, was both shocked
and impressed. The poem promptly slipped into almost
all the anthologies, or at least all in any way cordial to the
avant-garde.

To the very end of his career Stevens carried on with
his left hand this running battle against "rhetoric" and in
defense of "reality." But in this warfare as a rule he put
his naïve gusto behind him in favor of less raucous and

more profound expression. So in his last book, *The Rock*, appears the brief poem well entitled "The Plain Sense of Things," with its moving tribute to an austere beauty. The imagery is of autumn and also of a general decline in the vitality and perfection of things. All looks ordinary, bleak, dull. The leaves have all fallen; a blank cold has settled down; colors are dull; the chimney is leaning; the greenhouse needs painting. But, observes the poet, the imagination remains unimpaired, for it is exercised as much in imagining privation as in imagining opulence. He now dislikes the reflections in water that once so allured him. Instead, he prefers dirty, opaque glass, plain mud, a rat crawling across it. The lilies have all gone. The Pre-Raphaelites have gone. Very well, then, the imagination remains triumphant. For one must imagine poverty or disaster if it is to be truly known. The poem is terse, powerful, and typical.

V : *Some Major Themes*

STEVENS' compulsion to explore the relations of aesthetics and reality led him into many fruitful fields adjacent to this main concern: explorations of various art forms, of the physical world, and complexes in human emotions. It inevitably led him, also, into familiar provinces of metaphysical and philosophical speculations, a few of which he cultivated with much success in behalf of his poetry. At the very height of his powers he produced three poems of this nature which form something of a sequence and especially repay study, chiefly because all three are not only distinguished in themselves but elusive. These are "Chocorua to Its Neighbor," "Credences of Summer," and "The Auroras of Autumn." The first, being essentially theological, stands slightly apart yet in several ways is closely tied to the others by both its form and its content. All three are poems of fair length, comprising 130, 150, and 240 lines respectively. All are written in Stevens' normal verse line employed in unrhymed stanzas. In "Chocorua to Its Neighbor" he simply uses five-line stanzas. "Credences of Summer" employs the same stanza organized in strophes of three stanzas each. "The Auroras of Autumn" is divided into ten strophes each containing unrhymed triplets. The precise nature of the segmentation is, of course, less important than the formal construction of the pieces as a whole, which renders them odes in a modern manner.

All three works are alike in that each deals with a large abstraction, the first with a modern interpretation of theology, or of God, the second with the idea of complete spiritual gratification, a unity of mood unbroken by any discord or crucial division, the third with a theory harmonizing the human spirit in the presence of a world subject to both change and decay. Perhaps one should examine in connection with these three works a fourth poem, "The Rock," the title poem of Stevens' last volume. There is a wintry tone in *The Rock* that suggests the continuation of Stevens' symbolism from the seasons, and it may appear that here, with his specific concentration upon the aesthetic imagination, he resolves to his own temporary satisfaction the problems raised by his earlier studies in theology, in the fulfillment of man's emotional life, and in man's compromises in the face of inevitable frustrations. But the last major poem diverges considerably in imagery, form, and meaning from the preceding, and comparatively little would be gained by associating it with them.

Whatever value may be placed on "Chocorua to Its Neighbor," and the value should be high, it must almost certainly be regarded as one of the most extraordinary poems to be written in America. In certain respects its outlook is primitive, in others highly sophisticated. A mountain is selected as symbol for the idea of God, and all the long story of man's worship of mountains looms silently behind it. This particular address to the mountain is, however, the summation of much of Stevens' subtlest transcendental thinking. The mountain is not, of course, in any primitivistic way worshiped as a deity. It becomes the symbol for man's realization of divinity, especially as conceived by monotheism, although all speculations on the divine are in some measure contemplated. The word "God" is not used and no actual deity is named. Much is conveyed by implication. The mountain, especially as seen by night or toward dawn but still under the dominance of the morning star, evokes grave religious meditation. It is thus the immediate cause of the poem, the agent evoking an experience that itself lies in one of the most deep-seated chambers of the soul.

Stevens' conception of God is modern at least to the degree of being distinctly Emersonian. God is described as the ultimate abstraction and as "the self of selves." God is our largest thought, larger than our conception of cities, armies, or nations, although, as observations toward the poem's close remind us, these entities have themselves gone far to frame many of man's conceptions of the divine. To Stevens, the ultimate God must be single and the conception of a single man, like "one foot approaching, one uplifted arm." He is not created by a synod or a committee. A church must be a physical institution, but God is a vision and a mystery. The conception lies on the verge of the nothingness of the inconceivable, life in its most basic and elemental aspect. God must be personal because only persons create him. He is not of necessity the creator of life but is its eternal sustenance. Deity stands at the extremest limit of motion and conceivability; it is further symbolized by man's most intimate motion, breath; the luminous mountain in winter cold beneath its star is said to be human and to breathe. All three of the poems chiefly discussed in this chapter make much of the imagery of breath. This is one of the many ties relating them all to Buddhist thought and imagery. The mountain is human also in being not absolute in self-contentment, though it is ultimately all-powerful and serene. The poet accepts a contradiction here that flows into the system of his thinking as a whole. God is lonely in the vastness of space. Emptiness as well as repletion fills the universe. The mountain peak, superb in isolation, makes verbal confession of this weakness. Whereupon the poet, his neighbor, reasserts the majesty and fullness of the divine, man in this instance consoling God instead of God comforting man. God resembles the poet, as the poet resembles God.

God, we are told, exists because man wishes him to be. He is man-created but man's ultimate creation and in a real sense greater than man, for he is man's conception of a brooding life within the universe, the very idea of the sublime. Stevens explicitly acknowledges the modernity of his thinking. God he describes as man's brother, not as his father. He is that realization of the universe upon which man relies for his most vital sense of well-being, for his capacity to breathe freely and deeply in a world affirmatively conceived. He is, in fact, not only a conception but an ultimate condition of the soul's well-being, embodying man's greatest capacity for largeness and, like the mountain, vast, rugged, vital, serene.

Every line and word of this poem serves its serious purpose in creating the thought and emotional experience which Stevens desires. It is what major poetry should be, an entirely fresh realization of familiar experience, a powerfully new creation in a world socially known and already spiritually established. The grave beauty of its imagery and music, its quiet conviction and freedom from the rant and rhetoric so commonly mutilating our expressions of the divine nature, render it an almost unique work. "Chocorua to Its Neighbor" is undoubtedly art and a noteworthy contribution to theistic thinking. In none of his other works does Stevens deal at such length or so sympathetically with theism.

Some of the poem's further distinction arises from an objectivity when the work is read biographically. Several times Stevens, regarding theism as an outstanding achievement of the poetic imagination, takes the additional step of considering poetry as the art of the divine and divinity as its offspring. By a bold stroke in his argument, the poet becomes both the god-maker and, in a sense, the god, or creator, himself. So poetry becomes religion, or religion becomes poetry. This romantic, flattering, and somewhat blasphemous view has enjoyed wide currency in verse of the last hundred years, to the extent of becoming almost a vulgarism. Stevens' obsession regarding the central role of the poetic imagination in life frequently assumes the aspect of a religion. This outlook contributed the greater part of his own faith throughout the larger portion of his life. Yet in his dialogue with Mount Chocorua he nowhere forces the aesthetic viewpoint into the foreground. To each man his own deity; there are no invidious comparisons. The theological case remains unsophisticated by an argument from truth or from other equally irrelevant considerations.

"Credences of Summer" is another remarkably original

poem equally rich in its imagery and content. It contains much about summer but much more about credences. Here the credences are not theistic, as in "Chocorua to Its Neighbor," but relate to man's major satisfactions in life wherever they may be found. Summer, viewed in its most concrete and sensuous aspects, is quickly translated into its most general and abstract meanings, the landscape painter subordinating his naturalism to philosophical ideas relevant to nature but still more pertinent to the general ways of men. The poem, taking an intimate view of summer as its point of departure, proceeds to a study of the ideas of fruition and consummation. On this level it no more deals with summer in the naturalist's sense of the word than "Chocorua to Its Neighbor" deals with a mountain. The subject is any force seen at its zenith or apogee. The life of cities and nations is kept in mind as well as the life of the individual, viewed from all aspects, as, for example, the moral, intellectual, or social. There is an apotheosis of family life as seen in the social function of the marriage ceremony, the perfect development of life in father, mother, and children. Section six expounds fruition on both the physical and the spiritual plane, as a mountain is splendid both in the luxurious vegetation around its base and in the gleaming austerity of its rocks and snow toward the summit. The seventh strophe, while studiously abstract, contains powerful images relating to sexual experience. Elsewhere evidence appears of Stevens' favorite view that life comes to its highest focus not with the many but with the one, as sexual experience commonly envisages its ideal in a single, perfect person of the opposite sex. Summer is the fanfare greeting this perfection.

Such an ideal, Stevens insists, must be held somewhat aloof from the scrutiny of the realist. But even if perfection be an illusion, it proves to be a necessary illusion, a "necessary angel," to use his words in another connection. Fruition is both classical and romantic; classical because it excludes romantic restlessness, romantic because it demands an element of idealization or optimistic illusion. With considerable delicacy, the eleventh strophe introduces a sly overtone, the recognition even at the height of summer that perfection itself cannot last and that autumn chills hover in the near-by air. This fear is at first transient, as the note of some shy bird, half heard. Stevens still remains capable of strong optimism and a deep-seated gusto, a singer naturally endowed to celebrate summer and a man or a civilization at its apogee.

The final strophe paints the thought in more or less theatrical terms. The imagery suggests French culture of the baroque period in the seventeenth or eighteenth century, with its bright, mottled colors and "huge decorum," its rotund features, roseate complexion, and its worship of youthful happiness. Green and blue, related hues, are also among its symbolical colors, signifying the perfection of imagination upon a bright, windless day, as in Watteau's masterpiece, "Embarkation for Cythera." The characters in this artificial drama talk familiarly to one another, although the poet thoughtfully insists that the dramatist himself cannot hear their words. This indicates a nonintellectual quality in perfection or fruition; we think most keenly in the invigorating chill of winter, not in the delicious but enervating heat of summer. Language, the foremost vehicle of the intellect, belongs less to ecstatic spring or complacent summer than to the depression of fall and the austerity of winter, which, though possibly devastating, are also mentally exhilarating.

Admirable as it is, "Credences of Summer" is a less brilliant poem than "Chocorua to Its Neighbor" or "The Auroras of Autumn," but, curiously enough, it is an even more original one. The theme of absolute happiness has been less often treated with distinction in art and literature than the more dramatic themes of human deformity in comedy and human calamity in tragedy. In many instances, as in much pastoral poetry, the subject of pure happiness discourages imagination because of the temptation to an easy, sensuous naturalism evading life's complex realities. Joy is made to appear too easily accessible. The poet becomes not imaginative but fantastic. Schiller's *Hymn to Joy* has lasted far less well than the dramatic music which Beethoven composed in association with it. These reflections must place Stevens' brilliant praise of summer and of fruition in a peculiarly favorable light. His almost unique passion for the abstract saves him from both romantic illusion and sentimentality. The poem remains firm, its praise of felicity notwithstanding. Perhaps the gentle warning of the humorous bird perching on the bean pole in strophe nine contributes most to this unexpectedly gratifying result. This is indeed a good poem, but the static subject seems chiefly responsible for its aesthetic inferiority to a stronger and more vigorous work, its companion piece, "The Auroras of Autumn."

That no good thing lingers, that all things change, has been the lugubrious lament of artists for ages and from all quarters of the globe. The world, as Stevens observes, seems to come to a halt in summer. That is a season of the static, like winter; one of absolute fulfillment, the other of absolute privation. But if Stevens as a man loved happiness best, as a poet he loved the dramatic best and found himself peculiarly at home in celebrating the endless mutability of things. (The scholar of English poetry is likely here to recall the marvelous beauty of the two cantos of Edmund Spenser's unfinished seventh book of *The Faerie Queene* which are devoted to the pageant of Mutability.) Mankind as a whole thinks it has ideas and ideals reasonably fixed only to find them unsettled and the best laid plans of mice and men grown awry. As a poet of the twentieth century, Stevens became peculiarly conscious of the shift from one fortune to another, from one flag to another, and from one belief to another. One of the three major precepts in his long poem on the theory of aesthetics, "Notes toward a Supreme Fiction," is simply, "it must change."

On his wing of powerful imagination, Stevens easily flies far above the clichés and banalities of ordinary autumnal verse, stressing romantic melancholy and sensual despair, to an expression in many of its aspects amazingly Buddhist. "This is where the serpent lives," his poem begins, and continues for several lines to play upon the theme of the sinister monster totally new after shedding its former bright, glistening skin. The poem follows the theme of the one god who is also the creator and destroyer, the divine vindication of change, virtually the deity celebrated in Shelley's "Ode to the West Wind," but ultimately belonging not to the somewhat specious romantic Shelley but to the profound Sanskrit poets writing many centuries before. No single syllable in Stevens' poem actually demonstrates acquaintance with the Sanskrit in any form, but whether the ties as Stevens knew them were direct or accidental, it is certain that in both cases a common human chord is struck.

Stevens' poem varies in musical fashion the themes earlier announced in "Credences of Summer." Strophe one, as we have seen, is mythological, devoted largely to the Siva, or serpent, image; strophe two deals brilliantly with autumn not in its overfamiliar phase of fall foliage but in the seasonal changes observable on northern beaches by the sea, where wind and sky express so great a part of the change; a cold gale bleaches to white the boards of deserted cottages. The three strophes following deal with the slow retardation of excitement in family life as years pass by. The relation of parent and child cools. The father strenuously but vainly attempts to preserve the glamor and gusto of youth. Even his books no longer charm him. It is said of the aging mother that her necklace becomes "a carving not a kiss." These stanzas have a profound tenderness not often equaled either in Stevens' own writings or in those of other poets. The alleged honor of advancing years is depicted as an assumed brilliance, something enacted, a stage show, not faithful to reality. That life is basically tragic becomes the crowning reality, evoking art's most eloquent and convincing expressions.

But is this truly so, asks the hopeful poet? An indefatigable remainder of human courage is depicted as surviving, and though tragedy may surpass comedy in the magnificence of its art, even a flippant or moonstruck word is declared enough to deflect the bitterest tide away from human disaster. Death and defeat are not ultimate disasters. An innocence exists that refuses to surrender all life to destruction. In face of this innocence, the death of a man, of a nation, or of an autumn season may be no more than a sad song sung by a peasant mother to her sleepy child, to the accompaniment of an accordion. This homely image, at the conclusion of the eighth strophe, is especially tender and moving.

Yet particularly in its social context, the poem declares, life is today, as no doubt it always has been, menacing. The destroyers will come, as surely as man and his civilizations exist. The fatality is as certain as winter. The final strophe proposes again certain outlooks that, despite all catastrophes, may assist in the survival of the positive spirit in man. Actually, the poem passes here from an autumnal lament to a sober apotheosis. With a romantic fertility of imagination and a neoscholastic thirst for order, Stevens envisages four possibilities: unhappy people in a happy world; unhappy people in an unhappy world; happy people in an unhappy world; and happy people in a happy world. The first of these he casually proposes and temporarily sets by. (A technique suggesting art in process of creation, as though the reader looked over the creator's shoulder while he sat at his task, is eminently typical of Stevens, who deeply enjoys the fiction of improvisation.) The second proposition seems altogether too lugubrious, the fourth altogether too fantastic, like an *opéra bouffe*. The third appears unconvincing, pointing to a sentimental and rhetorical art ultimately repulsive. No, the best formula is that of the man who feels the dark force of autumn and of tragedy but who is not to be overwhelmed by life's disasters, whose forces are within and who would rather blame himself than the universe for his misfortunes. This is doubtless both sound psychology and sound theology, though romantic theology often neglected the solution as contrary to its own superficially considered optimism. Humanism finds the center of man's gravity in man.

Happily, the poem ends not with this rather dry yet eminently serious dialectic but with an allusion to "winter's nick." This final strophe is highly intellectual and reflective poetry, though not inartful in a poem devoted to the austerities of autumn. In the end autumn carries its message to the poet not from the hectic leaves but from the glistening sky. The northern lights, which give the poem its title, most brilliant in autumn, shed an aurora of brilliance and hope even upon a dying scene.

In several other poems, briefer but hardly less forceful, Stevens revolves these themes of the physical universe and the human predicament. Sometimes he does this with a keen sense of comedy. "Bantams in Pine-Woods," a little poem of ten lines, has been popularly known, one regrets to say, not for its acidulous comment on theology but for the virtuosity verging on nonsense in the first two lines:

> Chieftain Iffucan of Azcan in caftan
> Of tan with henna hackles, halt!

The image is of a brilliant fowl spreading its tail with an insulting pride, which provokes the speaker of the poem to chase it off with a few frightening cries. The allegory is as follows: the Oriental cock clearly stands for the theism that advances a knowable, universal god to tyrannize over mankind; the speaker, on the contrary, stands for the pragmatic New England Yankee who finds only arrogance in these Oriental gestures and discovers that the sages in question are to a wise man's eyes as petty as gaudy fowls inhabiting a darkly noble pine forest. A thinker edu-

cated beneath the sharp points of Appalachian pines is
unlikely to be impressed by such specious theology. To
him, to paraphrase Stevens, God is "the self within the
self." Though barely more than an epigram, the poem is
well worthy to rank beside the best that Omar, Attar,
Firdusi, or any of the chief Persian poets offer in comparison. And Fitzgerald himself in translating from the Persian employed no more exquisite or witty style.

"Looking across the Fields and Watching the Birds
Fly," a considerably longer and more elaborate and equally
imaginative effusion, extracts gentle humor from the often
humorless meditations of the Concord Transcendental-
ists. The lines describe the thoughts of a certain Mr. Homburg, of Concord, Massachusetts, whose name presents a
possible fusion of Hamburg and humbug and certainly
suggests the strong German background of New England
idealism. The work is ironic; quite clearly, too, Stevens is
more concerned with stating a case faithfully and imaginatively than in offering it for final decision. The tyran-
nical role here assigned to nature, viewing men not as men
but virtually as the unconscious mannikins of natural forces
or impulses, stands dangerously near a view of the poet
himself reflecting without divergence the various moods
and forces of landscape and nature. Mr. Homburg observes the natural forms as unconscious automatons of a
universal will, an indwelling power in nature. Nature ani-
mates all its creatures as the wind sweeps dramatically
across the marsh grass or as the blackbirds are driven in
unison by the gale. Is man's business a free quest for intellectual knowledge of these cosmic forces, for imaginative recreation of them, or must he forever, like the grass
and birds, remain unaware of any meaning in the winds

of destiny or even of the true prognostication of them? Does he make artifacts from nature or does nature make a slave of him? This is an imaginative and philosophical poem of some distinction, singularly precise in its statement of one of the transcendental views and deliciously ironic in its blend of humorous self-consciousness, objectivity, and, withal, a pervading seriousness.

Contrary to the thesis of Professor Homburg, nature, Stevens believes, is not enough to guide man or to account for him. Man is, ideally speaking, the artist who fashions himself by the use of nature. In this connection one more poem should be cited, "The Apostrophe to Vincentine." This early and distinctly lyrical work falls into four short strophes, each in contrast with the others. The first declares that Vincentine when naked looks small and thin in the great empty world of inhuman materialism. The second discovers her actually more sexually alluring when gracefully sophisticated by a colored dress. It is only then that the lover sees her most clearly as a brunette and dwells emotionally on the shades of her green, vernal dress passing occasionally into white. So man's imagination dresses the world itself in alluring colors. Nature is not what he finds but what he makes. The third strophe shows Vincentine for the first time in motion, among men and women, and vehemently talking. This marks a long step forward through the portal to social living. The fourth strophe states that the lover, attending to Vincentine's words, has penetrated her thoughts and feelings and at last come to know her as a true human being, a creature of will, imagination, and individuality. In thus becoming truly human, she even becomes, with a certain poetic license, divine. The physical has led to the spiritual, the earthy to the heavenly, the naked to the nude, the crude beginnings to the crown and justification of love.

In comparison with other Stevens poems, especially the three odes and the longer satire considered in this chapter, "The Apostrophe to Vincentine" may appear slight and, indeed, its doctrine is much more orthodox than surprising. But its thought is none the less vital and important, and in terseness and delicacy of expression the poem is hard to surpass. It shows Stevens as a true humanist, which, indeed, his theological poem, "Chocorua to Its Neighbor," and his philosophical poems, "Credences of Summer" and "The Auroras of Autumn," clearly indicate with use of a rhetoric vastly more involved.

VI : *Fantasy, Irony, Humor*

O F THE six poems examined in the preceding chapter, only one, "Bantams in Pine-Woods," can be described as predominantly humorous. Comic irony is of some prominence in "Looking across the Fields and Watching the Birds Fly." An elusive lightness of touch in "The Apostrophe to Vincentine" might easily lead to a conclusion that its author favored a comic outlook on life. These are the lesser poems in the group. "Chocorua to Its Neighbor" is wholly serious; so is "Credences of Summer;" only a single line in "The Auroras of Autumn," that concerning the "flippant conversation under the moon," lightens the pervasive gravity of that impressive and somber poem. These variations in mood naturally raise the question of Stevens' complicated orientation to the comic spirit and the degree to which he is committed to it. His critics themselves have taken sharply diverse positions— Robert Pack, for instance, describing his outlook on life in the most comprehensive terms as comic, whereas William Van O'Connor lays small emphasis on this phase of the poet's thinking. The subject holds considerable fascination and importance, though vexed to begin with by the various senses in which the word comic is commonly understood. Stevens' wit and urbanity raise a question which any critic worthy of the name must face, but not without some initial scrutiny of the terms themselves.

Our conception of comedy, a word even more elusive than humor, is almost inevitably conditioned by the use of the term in reference to drama. So far as concerns Stevens, this usage is generally of indirect value, except in relation to his two plays. "Three Travelers Watch a Sunrise" stands within the broad definition of tragedy, whereas "Carlos among the Candles" may be regarded as high comedy. It would be hard to say which is the more typical of its author. Where the word comedy is used of nondramatic writing, the meaning must chiefly lie in the description of an outlook upon life. Does a poem, for example, proceed from the comic spirit, the tragic spirit, or some other philosophy? The chief difficulty arises from the widely divergent variations of the comic outlook, which range from the supercilious smile to the convulsive guffaw. Generalizations have to be carefully guarded; it should be clear that by no means all cultures in their ripest and most developed forms reject tragedy, and the comic outlook cannot be restricted to any stage of civilization. Though "high comedy" belongs exclusively to advanced cultures, low comedy is by no means confined to primitive or naïve peoples. Broadly speaking, neither societies, individuals, nor artists view life consistently in these terms. None of us can live continuously on the plane of tragedy, sophisticated comedy, low comedy, or any other such exclusive outlook. Art distinguishes where life makes no clear distinctions. It should be added that the tragic outlook seems more circumscribed than the comic. Tragedy lacks the disparate moods into which the comic spirit falls. In describing a poet such as Stevens, the reasonable position is one of qualification. Does he stand closer to the comic or to the tragic spirit? The absolute will scarcely be expected.

Stevens' obvious eclecticism is part of his modernism. As a rule he does not concern himself directly with either the tragic or the comic spirit. His outstanding problem is more metaphysical than dramatic: the question what is reality and how does art participate in it simply bypasses the tragic-comic duality. His emphasis on a primitivistic view of tragedy as expressed in "Sunday Morning" and in "Esthétique du Mal" stands at one extreme; perhaps his light verse may be said to stand at the other. But a balance is with Stevens almost unconscious. Life held many problems for him but this problem, the choice between tragedy and comedy, does not appear as one of its critical dilemmas. Mr. Pack's repeated assertion in downright terms that Stevens' attitude is comic cannot, I think, be sustained. It is far better to say that over various types of the comic spirit he has, when he so wishes, a remarkable command. To consider all his work as falling within the sphere of comedy on the one hand perilously distends the definition of comedy and on the other hand does scant justice to a considerable number of his productions which are eminently grave. Here, as usual, the essence of clear thinking lies in insistence upon distinctions.

In these fields there are no general conceptions to which Stevens clung throughout his life. On the whole, *Harmonium*, with its vernal spirit, stands closer to comedy than any of his later volumes. There are some peculiarly tart, satirical, and bitter pages in his volume *Ideas of Order*, and a more direct and tragic approach is recognizable in the succeeding *Parts of a World*. Poems more or less satirical he wrote in all periods of his career and at any time his wit might sparkle perilously. He himself distinguished certain of his poems as satirical, or combining wit with seriousness, first of all because of their topical allusions in a critical spirit. It was, as we have seen, a type of poetry which he wrote supremely well but which he himself valued less than his more sober pieces.

The great majority of his pages are not intended to make us either weep, laugh, or smile. His work is less high-pitched than the master emotionalists of either dramatic or nondramatic verse—say, Christopher Marlowe or Emily Dickinson. But what should probably be regarded as his most accomplished poems, as "Esthétique du Mal" or "Owl's Clover," are overwhelmingly serious. His satire, as in "Owl's Clover," leans more to the earnestness of tragedy than to the mirth of comedy. In that poem one is more often reminded of satirical irony in Spanish thought from Quevedo and Cervantes to Goya and Dali than of any of either the more urbane or more homely types of comedy. Where fantasy is joined with seriousness, it is the seriousness that prevails. There seem in general to be two views of Stevens, equally erroneous. One finds him a sober victim of fastidious obfuscation, a perplexer to small purpose of problems in aesthetic philosophy; the other finds him to be a smart trifler, a sober and sophisticated comedian, at his best when he wins from his reader an amused smile. This is the view that finds "The Emperor of Ice Cream" no more than risible, and "Bantams in Pine-Woods" a mere playing with the sounds of words.

The truth is that—to be sure, with great artistic restraint —Stevens sounds profound depths of emotion and commands innumerable inflections of the comic spirit, from the bitterest irony to the most amused fantasy or relaxing gusto.

His fondness for self-mockery easily misleads an incautious reader to underestimate his true seriousness. Much of the humor which he deliberately directs against himself, as in the flippant titles of so many of his poems, is patently a shield to protect his own tenderness of feeling. The view must not be set down as romantic duplicity. It is the attitude of Chaucer, who rode last in the pilgrimage to Canterbury and allowed himself to be mistaken by most of his companions for a dunce, especially in matters of love. The attitude is not widely displayed in Stevens' work but stands out conspicuously on certain occasions. It becomes clearest in "The Comedian as the Letter C," where Crispin is the one figure in the poem and certainly is viewed with a comic spirit, as the name itself must imply. Crispin and the author alike are careful not to take themselves too seriously. They vaunt no personal tragedies. Yet their desire to avoid an unreal seriousness, or a romantic pretense of the tragic, may well be interpreted not so much as a renunciation of tragedy as a desire to keep the tragic sense pure and uncontaminated by the sensational, the melodramatic, the sentimental, or the ultraromantic. There is an exquisite sense of proportion and self-command in "The Comedian as the Letter C." Passion is largely abstracted. The last words of the poem raise the possibility that the poet has been subtilizing to little or no purpose. But it would be the height of the naïve to accept this suggestion as a true statement.

It is intended to qualify undue solemnity and to issue insurance against spurious melodramatics. If the poem is in any sense comic, and this may well be granted, it is high comedy, which admits bitter feelings and strong emotions, though it dispenses with the tragic purgation so clearly defined in "Esthétique du Mal" and "Sunday Morning."

The latter poem shares many qualities with high comedy. Its imagery conjures up a world of carefully guarded expression and elaborate sophistication. It also contains a most eloquent and virtually unsurpassed apology for tragic emotion. Stevens is in the end more an ironist than a comedian and more a high comedian than a *farceur*. He has, to be sure, given us some of the wittiest and most amusing poems in American literature. We should do ourselves an injury to overlook or minimize these gayer pieces. But we should do ourselves a greater injury if we overlooked his high seriousness and tragic force. Concluding that he commands a personal idiom in his wit, he is almost as witty as Oscar Wilde; and concluding that his tragic sense is also personal and attended by his metaphysical preoccupations, he is quite as truly serious as Matthew Arnold. Everywhere he maintains this classical balance between the extremes of emotional unrestraint and shallow entertainment, between a fanatical search for truth and an epicurean lust for pleasure. He takes scrupulous care that neither his moral earnestness nor his zestful gaiety runs away with him. His zeal for truth, for wisdom, and for beauty is sincere and quite easily might have become fanatic, were it not for his comedy; as his comedy might easily have seduced him into virtuosity and triviality had he not been so firmly established in his emotional and intellectual positions.

No picture of him can be adequate without some detailed view of his fantasy, his comedy, and the lighter aspects of his wit and irony. One may begin with his studies in the fantastic, with such a delicate piece as "The Worms at Heaven's Gate." This little poem of nine lines, as its title alone might suggest, has a Blakean appearance. It is mockery that is in no sense satire—a light, grotesque playing upon a string instrument. As always in poetry, it is the manner and not the matter which matters. The theme, taken literally, is dark, if not tragic. One by one the worms carry away the parts of the body of an exotic princess, Badroulbadour. Asterisks modestly denote the more intimate portions of her body. There are several levels of irony. The procession of the worms is given a triumphal character, worthy of the princess. They carry her out as though they were her chariots. And indeed they are engaged in a triumph, for they deliver her from the tomb to a species of immortality, bringing her, according to the title, to heaven's gate. As the phrase indicates, the ceremony marks a resurrection, which may be interpreted either literally, as the reunion of the body with the ever-flourishing magnificence of nature, or as the resurrection of the soul, to which the physical action serves merely as accompaniment. The wry humor belongs to a well-known type of comic expression. Dealing neither in exaggeration nor in understatement, the poet commits himself to nothing. He merely states in imaginative language one of the ironies of existence. The music is halfway between a liturgical chant and a macabre march; it is and it is not parody. Stevens especially enjoyed this elusive variety of fantasy and wit. "Cortège for Rosenbloom," a poem already discussed in another connection, elaborates as a lyric much the same thought that "The Worms at Heaven's Gate" condenses into an epigram.

Stevens, who enjoyed imaginative zoology as keenly as Picasso, possessed a fondness for the zoological world which marks the occasions for much of his comedy and light verse. "A Rabbit as King of the Ghosts" proves one of his most uncannily light and imaginative pieces, quite otherworldly as it establishes its focus within the animal kingdom. Like any good specimens in a bestiary, the animals are also in a measure humanized, so that the entire poem constitutes, by ironic inversion, a witty satire on the homocentric conception of the universe, if not on the outlook of the egocentric individual. Stevens' rabbit is brother to Chaucer's chanticleer. This rabbit is intoxicated with his own happiness and good fortune. He fancies the world made entirely for himself, thus becoming a vehicle for tragic *hubris*. He luxuriates in a perfect evening and sundown, with the delightful illusion, first, that the cat, his mortal enemy, is safely absent, and, second, that whereas the rabbit is swollen to gigantic size, the cat is merely a lightning bug in the grass. By the most poetic intimation, the reader is made to feel that, instantly after the poem's last word is heard, the bright-eyed cat jumps and seizes his much-deluded prey, the child of innocence and of daylight. Under the spell of sunset, moonrise, and twilight, the rabbit conjures up his unreal world of pure optimism and illusion. The fantasy and delicacy of the conception render the work equally poetry and comedy in a thoroughly legitimate sense of the words. There is really a death in the poem—off stage. The story is tragic but its conception is comic. Stevens' imagination is uncommonly happy here and his unassuming little poem is an unquestioned masterpiece.

As friend to much in modern art and especially to its alleged liberation of the imagination, Stevens found himself an avowed champion of the fantasy that he practiced so ably. He states his position in a poem, "Agenda," first published in *Smoke*, one of the "little magazines," but never included in one of his volumes, possibly because its author thought it too trifling. Nevertheless there is no reason to doubt the sincerity of its plea for a higher degree of fantasy among writers. It begins by mockery of those who pompously proclaim their practicality, and proceeds to some social-geographical paradoxes, as the wish that Boston should be near Key West, that Charleston should be in New York, and Shasta a cooling mountain of snow in the Bahamas. Orchestras should, perhaps, be turned upside down, dancers perform on top of their beds, and similar experiments made for the enlivening of our staid civilization! Earlier centuries, the poet reminds us, were much less set against imaginative experiment than our own bourgeois times. At the poem's close one feels that Stevens is on the side of the angels and against the sharply regimented "College of Heralds." The work is a plea for the liberation of the imagination in the name of fantastic comedy.

The comic spirit in Stevens, however, grows more typical and more in evidence as the ingredients of irony and satire are mixed more evenly. This condition appears in a little masterpiece of comedy and wit, "The Virgin Carrying a Lantern," a poem of three terse quatrains. Part of the humor is the fantastic rhyming, notably "egress" with "negress." This is a work of pure imagination and no naturalism. It begins with the sufficiently absurd pronouncement, "There are no bears among the roses." As the poem progresses, one finds its first line not impossibly an allegorical statement to the effect that no dark ravisher lurks in the garden which is about to be visited at night by a virgin carrying a lantern. But a Negress is present who suspects the worst. The whole poem has a Mozartian ring. One suspects a comic opera assignation, a protesting lady, and a Negress set as a spy. For some reason, the lover simply does not appear. Or should we take the protestation of innocence at its face value? There may even have been an outdoor convenience. This being a comic world, no decision in the matter is required. The poet gives us not a detective story but a miniature creation of pure delight, a gem sparkling with the light of a clear, cold comedy. Many of Stevens' more powerful poems are too profuse in ornament and detail to linger in the memory, whereas this trifle is almost impossible to forget.

"The Virgin Carrying a Lantern" smiles at the expense of conventional moralists; "The Doctor of Geneva" at the expense of intellectual pretension. The latter is the more typical of Stevens, as it is the more extended and developed work of irony. Possibly the poem on the doctor of theology or metaphysic was suggested to Stevens by a celebrated anonymous American primitive painting frequently exhibited in the Museum of Modern Art, representing a gentleman in dark formal dress and a lofty silk hat meditating on a beach festooned with prim waves, like white scalloped curtains. Much of the poem's irony lies in the respect which it avows for its ridiculous figure. The small philosopher in the presence of the sublime

forces of nature does not feel in the least overpowered;
possibly he is momentarily embarrassed; he is certainly
impressed; but he remembers his sound training in a bourgeois theology and metaphysics and braves his difficult
situation with dignity unimpaired. He shows his wisdom
by patting down his tall hat more tightly against the wind.
One of his reflections is that Racine or Bossuet may actually have rivaled the ocean in eloquence and grandeur.
Nature fails to overwhelm him because he is a scholar of
the magnificence of man. No statement is made to the
effect that the doctor is a crabbed dogmatist. After several
readings the student begins to suspect that he has here, as
so frequently in Stevens' work, a humorous self-parody
that is not in the least satire nor designed to demean its
hero. Could Stevens himself be the Doctor of Geneva?
It is a humorous possibility regarding one of the most
deftly written and amusing of his shorter poems. Calvinism haunted him, as it has long haunted Allen Tate, John
Crowe Ransom, and Robert Penn Warren.

This poem of moderate length leads naturally to one
of his more ambitious pieces, "Le Monocle de Mon
Oncle." As previously observed, this work smiles not at
pretensions in morality or intellect, but at sex and its
countless projections through the mind. It constitutes
Stevens' equivalent to T. S. Eliot's "Prufrock," with certain notable differences. Although each poem ridicules a
man in the decline of his powers, Eliot's poem stresses
the impotence of the entire social outlook of its victim,
whereas Stevens' more genially focuses upon the ironies
of sex, the mock hero more eloquent and excitable than
ever but decreasingly capable of realizing his desires.
Stevens' poem is narrower in its satire in that it stresses

the empty and inflated rhetoric of its hero, whereas Eliot's presents much broader areas of conduct to the reader's scorn. Stevens' style and possibly his theme are less distinctly "modern" than Eliot's. All this does not mean, however, that Stevens' poem is inferior; it signifies only that its humorous outlook is more concentrated. Though its own pretensions are not so great, the execution is truly remarkable; this was one of the earliest pieces in which Stevens fully matured his own vast powers in rhetoric. Smooth, eloquent, always civilized, witty, and urbane, "Le Monocle de Mon Oncle" is clearly a masterwork in high comedy.

Some dramatic and ironic contrasts in its style deserve notice. The hero employs lofty imagery, theological and historical. He invokes heaven. In describing him, the American poet recalls the aging poets of China who still persisted in writing of love, and further reflects on the sophisticated artifices used to prolong sexual attraction after the body itself has declined. Strung upon these thoughts is a wealth of imagery from animal and vegetable life and especially from the life of birds. Angels are contrasted with mules. We read of luscious and impeccable fruit contrasted with empty gourds that come with autumn and the fall. "A red bird flies across a golden floor." A pigeon that shows as heavenly blue against the sky is seen as pale white when it descends to earth. The poet has never known till now "that fluttering things make so distinct a shade." He hears the eloquence of the hero as the bellowing of a distended frog. In short, the pattern of imagery is brilliantly sustained and admirably conceived to produce the desired ironical contrasts. Notable, also, to the student of Stevens is the considerable frankness, though covered with a garment of baroque and flowing eloquence, with which the poet deals with sex. This quality persists in Stevens' verse almost to his last works and should be kept in mind in view of the austerity of much of his poetry, its strongly intellectual content and deliberated style. After the traditional manner of a Frenchman, Stevens is at once frank and polite. It is no exaggeration to describe him as a lusty poet and if he occasionally laments the autumnal season of sex, this in itself serves as further demonstration of what at first may appear a paradoxical statement. There is for him no conflict between the flesh and the angels. He and Omar would have understood each other.

It is further helpful to contrast his more openly satirical style with his more frequent irony-with-gentleness and to note how well are blended his sympathetic understanding and his somewhat acid disesteem. The reader must keep alert to weigh such nice shades of satire and opinion. As one of his tarter pieces may be cited, "Cy Est Pourtraicte, Madame Ste Ursule et les Unze Mille Vierges." The implausible subject titillated Stevens. He is perfectly fair to all concerned and it is obvious that whether or not he esteems the historical saint and her only semihistorical followers, he highly esteems the images of them all in art. Not only the title of this poem is French; its entire irony and humor, with realism preferred to a fictitious idealism, reminds us of French authors from Jean de Meung to Giraudoux. The irony is at the expense of Christian psychology. In historical terms, Abelard is esteemed more as lover than as pietist. Stevens' poem is based on a neat contrast. The saint recalls that she has decorated two shrines to her lover, Christ: one, in the church, ornamented with such respectable flowers as daisies, coquelicot, and snow-pale roses; the other, an impromptu, secret altar in the field, grossly adorned with radishes, grasses, and wild flowers. She fears that she has somehow offended her lover, God. But the poet generously proposes that to this God the second altar is at least as acceptable as the first. The poem whispers a prayer in behalf of a life in which sensuality plays a conspicuous part. At its conclusion we read that at least so far as Christian literature is concerned, "This is not writ in any book." The humor is humane but, so far as the orthodox are concerned, tart.

In 1950, in the little magazine *Wake*, many years after his poem on St. Ursula, Stevens published what may be regarded as a complementary piece, "Nuns Painting Water-Lilies." The comparison casts light on Stevens' almost habitual ambivalence. Again we have holy women seen through a world of art, with imagery from symbolic flowers. Humor is not wholly absent, I think, from the later poem, and its whole mood is much sweeter and less tart; there is less youthful asperity and a wiser gentleness and understanding. Again Stevens, reflecting on the Christian conception of chastity, views it as a limiting ideal; yet he no longer sees it as an impoverishing ideal or smiles at any duplicity or spot upon the petal of the flower. On the contrary, he gives thanks for the freshness and peculiar beauty breathed from this ideal and expressed in unforgettable paintings of the school of Fra Angelico. In his mature philosophy opposites may be true and their juxtaposition not ludicrous, as might appear to a rigid scholastic. Rather, in the temper of Kierkegaard, he finds himself writing a humorous but kindly apology for the monastic ideal, whereas the earlier poem befriended forces undermining it. His sophisticated humor encompasses the distance between satire and intelligent geniality. Wise at last as Thomas Hardy, he smiles no longer at men and women themselves but at life's own ironies.

Humor relies on inconsistency and delights in paradox, releasing the mind from smooth and facile clichés, the banalities of an imperceptive orthodoxy. It is this humor which enlivens and inspires Stevens' poetry, whether or not its immediate attitude be that of comic hilarity. In other words, the comic spirit must be celebrated and appraised not only for its own beauty and wisdom but for its rays cast into almost all corners of a poet's work. These conditions also account for the numerous likenesses in thought and expression in Shakespeare's comedy, *Twelfth Night*, and his darkest tragedy, *King Lear*. It would be an oversight to leave the view of Stevens' poems especially devoted to the comic spirit without a glance at the characteristics which his serious or almost humorless poetry shares with his lighter verse. In this regard the imagery of "Woman Looking at a Vase of Flowers" affords some happy instances. The emotional irony and complexity of this poem, its conjunction of sophistication with a tremendous energy in imagination, glances back upon the indubitably comic poems and illustrates how natural it is for a deeply imaginative writer to be also the master of the comic style.

In this instance the poem's subject is stated literally in its title. A woman is admiring a bouquet. But she is a brilliant woman, one in whose mind "the little owl" of the imagination flies. The violence in the brilliant colors of the flowers suggests to her "thunder upon the piano," the crude grandeurs of sun and sky, clouds becoming braided girls, the sea pouring its massive water over rocks, the beating of the wind. All of summer and its fruits springs into her thoughts. To the literal mind these are violent associations. To such the disparities might appear comic or even be found sheer nonsense. But the imaginative mind is capable of discovering deep seriousness in thoughts that in the unimaginative arouse either a misdirected sense of comedy or a gratuitous feeling of disinterest or contempt. The comic spirit is the spirit of liberation. Passing through its own domain, a smiling and fruitful lowland, it may enter into the superb scenery of both philosophical and emotional tragedy. It would be a great error to suppose Stevens the humorous poet another being from Stevens the tragic and highly serious poet; for a deeper scrutiny reveals them as one.

VII : *The Nature of Art*

WE HAVE seen that throughout his career as a writer
Stevens lived under the compulsion of exploring the
theory of art in relation to his theory of reality. So pronounced was this attitude that in various ways almost all
his other branches of consciousness were associated with
this parent stock. Thus he conceived the idea of God as
the supreme creation of poetry, civilization as the ripen-
ing of fruitful thoughts regarding art and their implemen-
tation in practice, and all sound relations between people
as the result of imaginative thinking that under peculiarly
felicitous conditions blossoms into art. Art is simply the
finest appreciation of life. We have found that these ideas,
which narrowed the horizons of many nineteenth-century
aesthetes, herding them into a cult of sterility, orientated
Stevens in a manner greatly stimulating to his mind and
poetry. Although nearly all his poems bear marks of his
philosophical obsession, most of the best of them reach
out into other areas of thought and sensibility. The image
suggested is almost inevitably that of the tree. Its trunk
or stem is the parent thought. And as most persons find

the magnificence of the tree rather in its leaves, flowers, and fruit than in its stem, so most of Stevens' readers find the true magnificence of his poetry in its lyric leaves, its blossoms of humor, and its fruits of thought and tragic insight rather than in its speculations on art, reality, and imagination. Still, the shining consequences of his compulsion can hardly be as rewarding as they are if the stem from which they rise is a negligible thing. His poems explicitly devoted to the aesthetic experience are often of great merit and must hold a prominent, though I think not a dominating, place in any appraisal of his work.

These productions range from trenchant aphorisms to moderately long verse-essays. Most of his collections of aphoristic poems, such as "Like Decorations in a Nigger Cemetery" and "Variations on a Summer Day," even when they contain a great wealth and diversity of material, will be found to be meditations on his favorite theme of the imagination, dominating him even more than the same theme dominated Coleridge. Among his longest pieces devoted explicitly to this subject are "Notes toward a Supreme Fiction" and "An Ordinary Evening in New Haven." In the most extended of his poems, "The Comedian as the Letter C," he is obviously capable of smiling broadly at himself. Even the titles of some of his longer poems devoted to speculations on aesthetics reveal this humorous proclivity, as "Academic Discourse at Havana" and "Extracts from Addresses to the Academy of Fine Ideas." This general group naturally constitutes the most difficult section of Stevens' writings, those which are the most astringently didactic in tone and as a rule the driest in style—perhaps the most intellectually substantial works but questionably the most perfected as poetry. These are the poems that require for most persons the most studious rereading, are the most difficult to recall in detail, and come the least fully into the light. The reader of Stevens should, accordingly, not begin with these pieces; nor did Stevens begin to write most of them until he was himself well advanced in years. His longest reflective poem in *Harmonium,* his first volume, "The Comedian as the Letter C," differs widely from later work on much the same theme. It is warm, witty, close to narrative verse, almost anecdotal, a transparent autobiography of the poet and his style rather than a verse-essay.

There is no trifling in the later long poems and all are rewarding. Built up as a rule as a sequence of shorter poems, or strophes, they undoubtedly contain some of his most substantial work. But few of them will be analyzed in detail in this book, for they are the least useful poems for the student first approaching Stevens, and the present study is designed as in introduction to his work, not as an appraisal of all its parts or as a final word on the subject. This chapter analyzes his aesthetic philosophy chiefly by reference to a few of his brilliant shorter poems. The discussion here will be of his more general ideas in this area; the succeeding chapter examines his psychological analysis both of aesthetics and of other aspects of thought and experience. The progression in general will be from the simpler to the more complex statements. For, his nuances of expression to the contrary, the core of his thought in these briefer poems is as a rule sufficiently simple.

A not too difficult statement of his faith in the efficacy of art appears in "Angel Surrounded by Paysans," selected as the final poem in his eloquent volume *The Auroras of Autumn.* A skeptical "countryman" asks if there is a wel-

come at the door of poetry "to which no one comes."
"The necessary angel" replies in the affirmative. The
poem's implication is that art, or the aesthetic imagination, is the necessary angel. But angels are no longer supernatural beings, for they have lost their glory, or their
aureoles, in the modern world. They are no more the
great princes of heaven, the stars no longer attend them
as courtly menials. Instead, the modern angels interpret
the stars for the needs of the human imagination. Today's
angels are simply the manifestations of man's imagination,
elucidating his ordinary daily life with miraculous shafts
of light. In words that are more like music than common
words and images more like dream than common actuality, they disclose the depths of comedy and tragedy. One
may still speak of angels, for these ministers of light have
only an impalpable being, half seen, half unseen, the
mysterious messengers of a spiritual understanding. All
works of art are such angels, that is, mysteries, beyond
strict definition or critical analysis. This poem is exquisitely
composed, giving concrete illustration to Stevens' abstract
proposition that sound art can never be obvious. Any
intellectual analysis must seem sadly cold beside the religiously inspired beauty of Stevens' image and phrase.

Slightly more conventional in its outlook is "A Postcard
from the Volcano," where, as often, Stevens supplies a
title ironically underestimating the true seriousness of his
purpose. His sagacity instructs him that of all evils pretentiousness is most to be avoided. This particular volcano
is modern life, although the meaning of the image is nowhere explicitly declared within the poem itself. The
theme is the familiar thought that art best carries to posterity the true image of its own times and reality. The

sensitive flesh is decayed; only dry bones remain. But the masters of the imagination have left true images for posterity. The world of Stevens' times is here presented as a mansion in a sad state of dilapidation, pale and gutted, its "shadows peaked to white." Nevertheless, splendor alights even here, no doubt through the mastery reached by modern artists, for the ruined mansion is in the last words described as "smeared with the gold of the opulent sun." Its artists have preserved it to memory, giving even to its sky "a literate despair." All the intricate beauty of imagery and emotion notwithstanding, the core thought of this poem remains simple and familiar.

Like the composer of a fugue, Stevens delights in turning an idea round about and examining it from different angles. In "A Postcard from the Volcano" he views art in the light of the future; in "Large Red Man Reading" he sees it in the ghostly half-light of the past. This is a poem of supposition and lost opportunity. Nothing is more common than the failure of society to recognize its seers and prophets in the time and place of their appearance. Or, to state the case somewhat differently, society requires time to reflect upon them until it has mastered their idiom and true meaning. This the history of almost any art shows; or such, at least, is the view familiarly received. Stevens constructs his poem upon this base. He imagines ghosts rising from their underworld to acknowledge the undying power of the poet, who in the essential form of his art is more than ever alive. Stevens' color denoting the imagination is commonly blue. Here the title describes the poet-seer as "red," the intention being the contrast between the undiscerning world, or at least the world that discerns so tardily, and the robust and ever-living poet, red being the alarming evidence of his strength. The ideal poet expounds to men the value or meaning of their most familiar experiences, their pots, pans, and common garden flowers. To their vapid life he gives color and reality. The poem's ghostly imagery is, of course, only incidental to its basic idea. As Dante declared, many who are living are pale ghosts and many of the dead are still vividly alive. The poem's proposition is relevant not only for the past but for present and future.

All art, Stevens believes, is form and all form a certain measure of abstraction. A society without art or ideas is a community without form. This is the transparent meaning of Stevens' popular little poem "Anecdote of the Jar," beginning, "I placed a jar in Tennessee." No particular ill is, of course, intended regarding that centrally located state in the Union. On the contrary, the "I" may well be taken to signify the spirit of art in America and the choice of Tennessee may refer to the group of highly imaginative writers who somewhat abruptly arose in Tennessee early in the present century, chief among whom were the Nashville "Fugitives." Art had come to a land hitherto much of a wilderness, aesthetically considered; by its interpretative and illuminating power it brought order into what had been previously chaos: "The slovenly wilderness" was transformed by the nobility of human understanding. The image from ceramics is especially felicitous, for in almost all cultures ceramics best represents the essence of design, an atomic power within the mind. It is also elemental in the sense that it is the art of the human hand applied to clay that is part of the common earth. Stevens was thoroughly cognizant of the importance of ceramics in general design and of the revival of this most ancient art in the

early twentieth century, both in terms of modern crafts-
manship and of imaginative scholarship in past cultures.
This was also a part of the neoprimitivism of Barlach and
Picasso. It likewise accompanied improved studies of the
Orient. A jar is placed in the center of the stage in Stevens'
play with Oriental characters, "Three Travelers Watch a
Sunrise."

Also, early in his career he composed a poem, "Bowl,"
published in *Others*, 1916, and presumably written at
much the same time as his drama. Possibly he thought
this little poem too facile, too close to Victorian idealism,
or he may have considered it inferior to the more austere
poem on the jar in Tennessee, which in many respects it
resembles. In any case, it was not included in any volume
during his lifetime. Nevertheless, it is an astonishing epigram and for its reprinting in *Opus Posthumous* we should
be grateful. It strikingly symbolizes his conception of the
world as known best through art. "For what emperor," the
poem asks, "was this bowl of earth designed?" The word
"earth" is used here in two senses, its lesser meaning signifying the potter's clay, its larger meaning, the globe of
earth itself. The poet imagines the world as a Chinese vase
on which the forms of animal and vegetable life are
painted, along with the sun and moon and human beings,
naked or clad in their bright dresses. The allusion to divinity may be somewhat Tennysonian, but the value of the
whole both aesthetically and intellectually is, to say the
least, considerable. It would be hard to find a symbol expressing more adequately Stevens' conception of the
world and human life as known most fully through the
arts. Nor should the theistic outlook, I think, be overlooked, in view of Stevens' own metaphysical poems, such

as "Chocorua to Its Neighbor," or his speculations that God is the ultimate creation of the poetic mind. This early poem lacks its author's usual distinction in phrase. It by no means lacks his high powers in the poetic symbol.

Stevens speculated on the relations between form and energy, expression and passion, in art and life. To his thinking, an emotion is best controlled when it is clearly imagined and is conveyed only when it is expressed, which is to say, through art. Formlessness is weakness and sterility; form alone is strength. Such thoughts must have strong appeal to any inspired formalist in art, as J. S. Bach, although to the philistine mind such emphasis on form possibly seems pedantic. On several occasions Stevens arranges his own thinking along these familiar paths. An instance occurs in "Stars at Tallapoosa," expressing the luminous geometry of artistic form. To Stevens as humanist, the stars are not in the sky but exist as realities in the human imagination, where, at least at the moment of his writing, they signify the thoughts just expressed: the clear, cold, unemotional purity of artistic form. On such guiding threads are the poet's warmest pictures of life woven. The poem has admirable eloquence. The spiritual geometry of the stars is preferred to the geometric patterns of the melon flowers or the insects' webs. The same thought found in "Anecdote of the Jar," to the effect that art's interpretation of the wilderness reduces the slovenliness of the wilderness to order, in other words, that chaos becomes order when understood, is expressed in "Stars at Tallapoosa." The moist earth-lines and fluid contours of the waves are contrasted with the lucid patterning of the stars and their arrowlike shafts of light. Pleasure itself is equated with the "nakedness" of the stars. Men have too

often forgotten these elemental lessons of art, failing to
realize that rigid form, economical as the precise movements of an athlete, alone conveys the most powerful feeling: "the lost vehemence the midnights hold." The pure
geometry of the stars even harmonizes with the combus-
tible tropical violence. There is, perhaps, no great novelty
in the idea but it is here brilliantly conveyed. Intellect, as
so often in Stevens, is transfigured into pure poetry.

He seldom doubts the value of artifice, though he repeatedly confesses, in the middle portion of his career, his
own excesses in virtuosity. In "The Comedian as the Letter C" he accuses himself of moments of excessive rhetoric. But in "Two Figures in Dense Violet Night" he
champions the utility of a witty, formal speech. The poetic
language of wooing, with its extravagant, sophistical, formal utterances, seems to him wholly desirable and de-
fensible. In this poem a woman rebukes a man for his failure to woo her in sufficiently eloquent terms. With the
intellectual values of language she is little concerned; but
her instinct tells her that Don Juan will be eloquent; the
great lover will be also the great master of verbal artifice.
Even if a lover commands at best only a simple rhetoric,
he must use that. No matter what the literal content, the
forms of language themselves will be gracious to her ear.

Stevens' poetry presents many other aesthetic considerations in broad terms, as, for example, some of the primary aspects and problems of modern art. Time has various significations in his evaluation of art. In "Recitation
after Dinner," a poem later to be discussed in some detail,
he gives a truly remarkable defense of the high value of
tradition. In other pieces, as "Mozart, 1935," he dismisses
his emphasis on tradition to champion the cause of mo-

dernity. The poem, somewhat quizzically bearing the name of the great composer, shows Stevens' awareness of the dual aspect of the problem of tradition and innovation. Elsewhere he asserts the importance to the artist of the initiative that saves him from writing in a manner of twenty years past. With his keen historical sense, so vividly cxcmplified in "Owl's Clover," he realizes the artist's need to express the problems of his own age. "Mozart, 1935," acknowledges the eternal greatness and freshness of the master, with warm allusions to concerto and divertimento, showing that he wishes Mozart's music to remain prominent on concert programs of any decade. But he realizes also the need for a strictly contemporary music, a new idiom, product of the endless unfolding of new forms. The pianist today should play the moderns perhaps even more than the classics. With his customary skill, Stevens contrives to make an attractive poem out of an idea that in its bare form approaches a commonplace. The poem escapes the commonplace because of its refinement of details and its abundant evidence that the poet possesses superior understanding of more than one musical idiom. And even if the central thought be commonplace, how much sagacity lies in it!

A much more elaborate statement in the description and defense of modern art is to be seen in his topical lines "Reply to Papini." This Italian scholar had composed in support of a papal pronouncement a reactionary attack on modern art, the familiar gist of which is that modern art is obfuscation and that poetry should be clear, popular, easy to read, optimistic, and consolatory. To this Stevens replies that the Fascist aesthetics is sterile and that truth lies in quite an opposite direction. Significantly,

Stevens states his position without making any special apology for modern art or modern times and even without concluding these to be essentially different from any other. His assumption, as in "Large Red Man Reading," is that poets always lead mankind to new awareness and that the process of poetic instruction is frequently a long and hard one for the public, who are their pupils. The way to heaven, which is faith's way, Stevens describes as relatively easy in comparison with the way to understanding, a part of which is art's way. Moreover, Papini notwithstanding, art deals more happily in intimations than in statements. A poem may have an intellectual core, but by virtue of being a poem it must have intimations and luminosities beyond the reach of the intellect. Art may be to a degree planned by the mind, but over and beyond these disciplines are the artist's inspirations, the all-important overtones, the indescribable nuances. These will not at first be easy for the consumers of art. They must be long digested. Or, to change the image, any art to be firm must also be hard. The truly great piece of music, even if it seems comparatively simple, as witness many pieces by Mozart, will reward the most intensive study and spiritual discipline on the part of its performer. The great poem must necessarily present similar problems. No matter how alluring its surface, its depths will be reached only by much labor. Stevens pleads with the champion of a Fascist parody of democracy to recall his proper place as champion of the great civilization of Italy. In substance, Stevens accuses Papini of selling cheap ware to the public. There is moral nobility in his charge and grave dignity in the moderation with which it is urged. The American states his case with wit, imagination, sincerity, and an aristocratic elegance of phrase that distinguishes his writing from the traditional savagery of satire. Whatever else may be said of it, "Reply to Papini" will long be memorable. Stevens accuses Papini of reducing the standards of art to "the politics of property." But the true poet is a daystar, even going before the philosopher in envisagement of things to come.

Writing in the earlier years of the twentieth century, Stevens could hardly avoid a keen awareness of the new areas being claimed by the modern artists, especially the painters, sculptors, and musicians. Being a man of the richest culture, he knew these arts, of both past and present, remarkably well, entertaining a distinctly cosmopolitan view of them. His intense interest in basic problems of art and the imagination also assisted him in holding such views. Stevens was not alone a verbalist, like Dylan Thomas. His vital interest and deep understanding where modern arts are concerned are reflected in a considerable number of poems, and in none more conspicuously than in his witty "So-and-So Reclining on her Couch," a notable study on the tendencies of modern art toward abstraction.

The imagery of this piece presents the modern artist and his model, not without shrewd overtones describing the modern lover and his mistress. The woman appears in each case something of a utility. She lies nude on a couch. Studying her, the artist discovers the abstraction of her form. Three aspects of the case are postulated: the woman as flesh-and-blood actuality, or as thing; the idea, or abstraction of the woman, which signifies the artist's understanding, the essential meaning of her form; and, finally, the art work, the painting, which, with the aid of all practical considerations of materials and technique, in due time appears on the canvas. Himself using the language of abstraction, the poet terms these three aspects projections A, B, and C. A lies on the couch; B floats, with "gothic" imagination, in mid-air; C is the completed work of art. Abstraction in art is explained here as demanding freedom from rhetorical irrelevancies, called merely gestures. In the general appreciation and experience of life, A and B suffice. A person commonly lives without those valuable aids which, at intervals, finished art provides. At the end of the poem the speaker courteously bids good-bye to Mrs. Pappadopoulos, the model and the mistress having been grasped in their appropriate meanings.

This is a poem about ideas and aesthetics, not on the more refined and ideal social relationships. It affords a fair and witty commentary on physical relationships, but a much more searching one on the ideas and processes of the modern artist, or, more properly, on the artist of any age. But the aesthetics of the piece seem especially agreeable to our own highly critical and self-conscious times. The poem shares much of Matisse's grace and Picasso's vigor. Both these artists, of course, stood high in Stevens' esteem. This *jeu d'esprit* is placed in *Transport to Summer* immediately before "Chocorua to Its Neighbor," and but one page removed from "Dutch Graves in Bucks County." The juxtaposition of such a slick bit of comedy betwen two such masterpieces in the serious vein points to the scope of Stevens' poetic genius.

Another memorable poem closely related to painting rewards examination as typical of Stevens' powers, again showing his conjunction of sophisticated wit and well-controlled sensuality. "Floral Decorations for Bananas," one of his most robust effusions, is a versified essay on taste which clearly owes much of its origin to still-life painting. It depicts decorations in a prim dining room of the upper middle class. Maybe the room is in the house of the uncle celebrated in "Le Monocle de Mon Oncle," for it begins with address to an imaginary and romantic "nuncle," who is clearly confused on sexual matters, as well as on the relations between life and art, nature and artifice. In all respects but one the room is in an eighteenth-century style, virginal, affected, precious, fit only for young ladies "in primrose and purl." Into it and apparently to the center of the table someone has brought a bunch of bananas, which suggest only tropical heat, violence, brutality, or even bestiality. The poem consists of two pairs of stanzas. The first pair, describing the precious room, is good, but the second, describing the torrid tropics, obviously constitutes the climax and stands among Stevens' most inspired flights of poetic rhetoric. All amorous verse, Stevens shrewdly intimates, is in a sense floral decorations for bananas.

That even in dealing with his favorite general subject this intellectual poet is not always intricate or dark appears in a short poem with a quite conventional attitude, redeemed for poetry by the considerable wit of its style. "Loneliness in Jersey City" reflects the all too familiar attitude of the modern poet complaining of his society and commiserating with himself. This is the nearest Stevens ever comes to self-pity and it is certainly not dangerously near. The piece deals not with art but with the artist. Jersey City is here assumed to be one of the more dismal of America's industrial hells. The poet finds himself in a hotel there (possibly returning from abroad), in room 293, with a window but nothing that pleases him to see from it. To be sure, William Carlos Williams has composed some of his outstanding and most exhilarating poetry using just such ordinary or even extraordinarily sordid material. But Stevens is more fastidious. With the eye of the satirist, he looks down upon a community so unimaginative that, in his own words, its members cannot distinguish between a deer and a dachshund. The community has its religion, for there are several churches, but its Sundays are as drab as its weekdays. People appear as flat as the cobblestones in the street. Many are well-to-do, for they flash by in large automobiles, but they have little music that rises above the concertina, that debased accordion, which is played without the peasant flair extracted from such an instrument, say, in Poland. The poet and his art are not appreciated. In Jersey City, it seems, imagination is defunct.

A general retrospect of Stevens' commitment to place leads to a paradox in aesthetics such as he himself found peculiarly arresting. His quest for an unrestricted power of imagination leads him to specific circumscriptions of the imagination. For the ideal poet he postulates a command of any given situation; yet to each situation the poet is irrevocably attached. He supposes a mind in warm imaginative relation to whatever weather-changes life's conditions present, alluring or repellent, good or evil, fair or foul. One stands close here to an Oriental ideal of contemplative composure, the spirit alert, the will in smooth adjustment with circumstance. This outlook is best defined by the Chinese characters in his play, "Three Travelers Watch a Sunrise," and in the remarkably revealing poem, "Extracts from Addresses to an Academy of Fine

Ideas." Of all his works these have the strongest flavor of an Oriental aesthetic and also the strongest statement of an outlook upon experience focusing the imaginative powers on given intersections of time and place. This best defines his aesthetic discipline. Hence he writes: "The law of chaos is the law of ideas."

VIII : *The Psychology of Art*

CERTAIN of Stevens' poems, as those examined in the foregoing chapter, present the reader with some difficulty because a fairly familiar idea has been refined by a great subtlety of language. In many other instances, in addition to the imaginative style, the ideas on art themselves are of some psychological depth. To poems of the second variety this chapter is devoted, while the succeeding chapter deals with some of his psychological insights less intimately associated with his aesthetic theories.

"Montrachet-le-Jardin" is a typical poem of some profundity and a fair proportion of difficulty. Its strength lies in part in its semidramatic quality. The central symbol is a poet-hero whose physical body suffers imprisonment and whose soul feels still more deeply imprisoned in a culture predominantly hostile because prosaic. Yet because he is the hero, a man of imagination, he is essentially a free man. According to the poem's chief tenets, no reason exists why his imagination should not be ethical, theological, or even political, but the instances given toward the poem's close are chiefly Stevens' familiar examples of

moods of the spirit symbolized by nature. The piece, despite its dramatic quality, is a psychological meditation.
Its insight springs from its dialectical form of illustration.
The thinker pursues his ideas to such a point that he is
able to illustrate them with concrete examples.

With his love for the recondite, Stevens has little use
for the downright dramatic monologue in Browning's
manner. Nor does he generally allow more than a glance at
an historical incident. In this instance there is a compro-
mise, or at least a pronounced eclecticism. On the one
hand, the poem presents the dramatic monologue of a
prisoner seeking a solution to his life, which suffers bitterly
hostile external confinements. On the other hand is the
statement of general ideas which renders the story of the
prisoner purely symbolic. The physical must not fetter the
free play of the metaphysical. For seven stanzas, or as the
work is set up on the pages of the *Collected Poems*, for the
first page, the prisoner appears to be speaking; then for
sixteen stanzas, or the next two pages, the first personal
pronoun disappears and we have a meditation on "the
hero;" with the twenty-fourth stanza, or the beginning of
the fourth page, the first personal pronoun abruptly reap-
pears and its force is steadily felt until the poem's final
stanza, where the pronoun occurs with special emphasis.
This ambivalent technique is followed in several other
of Stevens' longer poems. Nothing is left to accident in a
work of art by Wallace Stevens. All such conditions are
calculated. In the end we see the captive as a free man,
who has built a garden within his wilderness.

In many ways the poem follows lines of thought wholly
familiar to the reader of Stevens' works. Especially typical
is the emphasis on individuality. The poem's hero has at

one time dreamed of a Terra Paradise, which signifies a world focused on values conceived socially. But the hero has been forced into a predicament symbolized by solitary confinement. In this state he has learned self-reliance. Social life, signified by the "bastard chateaux," and sexual life, by the phrase "smoky demoiselles," cease to constitute centers of gravity. He has become the true philosopher, nourished on fact, on a treasure of virtue ascetically maintained. Stubborn thought has taught him a reconciliation of the views of the "root-man," that is, the physical man, or the average citizen, with the "superman," sophisticated and philosophically informed. He further reconciles the primitive with the highly cultivated, and "the salty skeleton" of the intellect with the emotion's "licentious violet and lascive rose." The religious world of Asia, marvelous as it was and in a certain sense self-adequate, no longer suffices for a society craving a new mythology. This, the poet declares, is the mythology of modern poetry and the modern imagination, reality as illumined by the poet's words.

Although giving an impression of spontaneity and improvisation, the poem, like so many other of Stevens' works, also savors of dialectic. In illustration of the liberating imagination he advances five specific "items," each in essence a poem in itself, condensed to a score or a dozen words only. This is Stevens' customary aphoristic manner incorporated in the style of a comparatively long poem. The first "item" describes the sensation of newness evidenced in the freshness of dawn, with the cry of cock and bird and the radiance of the sun, all focused upon one reality. The second item concerns the vagueness of the wind; the third, the sensation of perfection and fulfillment experienced at the sight of green fish swimming among green weeds in green water; the fourth item finds in the clear fall of a refreshing cataract an illumination of fact following fact in an unbroken sequence of insights into reality; the fifth item is the conviction, familiar to Oriental religion and often recapitulated by Stevens, that the breath is the center of life and of the senses, in a mystical sense the very essence of the soul. These are all gratifying speculations. The sudden turn in the very last words of the poem is again typical of Stevens' dramatic style. He seeks truth and feels that he has found it but insists on freedom from dogmatism. He has defined his hero of the hour, but perhaps all heroes are not alike.

> I affirm and then at midnight the great cat
> Leaps quickly from the fireside and is gone.

The words exhibit the distance between the prosaic statement of their bare intellectual content and the poet's insight and eloquence. There is something catlike in the universe, wherein truth cannot be domesticated. A dog may be trained but not a cat. Life has its way of escaping control, even by the most inspired "hero," or artist.

The artist's insight, Stevens observes, is intuitive. Considerable verbal virtuosity is required to express the five "items" of insight given at the conclusion of "Montrachet-le-Jardin." Stylistically considered, this is a long, richly overladen work in Stevens' best rhetorical manner, where every syllable is weighed and verbal play remains extremely brilliant. The opposite manner is achieved in "Dinner Bell in the Woods," written in 1954, a poem in his most mature style, amazingly "naked" in its symbolic statement. The core-meaning is a sense of complete contentment, of idyllic happiness and satisfaction. The image is of a clear-sounding bell rung by a buxom mother to assemble children at a picnic in the woods. All the poem's imagery confirms our conviction of clarity, serenity, deep contentment. There are only eight lines. The simplicity of the clear, bell-like tone, entirely Oriental in its aesthetics, cannot easily be matched in our literature. An utterly unassuming poem, like a Tang clay figurine, by magic attains religious profundity. It presents precisely the opposite type of "difficulty" from that found in "Montrachet-le-Jardin." One is difficult because of its complexity, the other, because of its simplicity.

Further ideas on aesthetics are memorably expressed in one of his most frequently cited poems, "The Idea of Order at Key West." The poem has a body followed by a postscript, as a yacht carries its tender astern. The main section of the work develops the familiar idea that nature in essence is not what is seen but what is imagined and felt, is not, when viewed in any profound sense, an objective thing but rather the raw material for the poetic imagination. Perhaps it does have a spiritual reality of its own but for us the interpretation of its meaning depends primarily upon an act of reconstruction. Nature becomes reality when we see it at once truthfully and symbolically. The thing itself is always an inner reality, appearing differently to all persons, but organized to some extent for the social imagination by the artist, who speaks to many men and for them. Like the architect, the artist designs for the public. For him the imagined world is the real world, or at least emphatically so for the time and mood of his conceptions. The artist, in short, orders his world and ours. Out of the bewildering welter of the landscape itself he constructs the essential image, the meaningful work. This idealistic view of aesthetics constitutes the body of the poem.

The coda makes an artful and natural appendage and is, in fact, the more original and brilliant part. It affirms that any work of art, as a song rising from the inspiration of a certain tropical scene, will inspire the capacity for fresh organization and imaginative thought in all who rightly experience it. As far as the poem has a narrative, it supposes auditors enjoying a lyric with a strong rhythmical movement sung by a woman on a tropical beach beside the rhythmical breaking of the waves. Afterward the auditors are confronted by a harbor with lighted boats lying at anchor. Having heard the song, they are themselves attuned to the imaginative mind which creates order from the raw materials exciting it. The boats and their lights, the contours of the harbor, the water and sky, take on a new order and meaning. They find themselves living in the heightened domain of the poet, artist, and musician. Not the least value of this extraordinary poem is its capacity to unite three artistic insights, those of poet, painter, and musician, into the larger realm of art itself and the imaginative mind. The work is dedicated to the "blessed rage for order." It praises nature and the arts alike, concluding with the affirmation of the imaginative way of life, for both the creator and the enjoyer, for the one who actually embodies his insights into works of art and for the one who both enjoys such works and silently thinks along imaginative paths.

Contrary to the views of a decadent aesthetics, art may state facts objectively and embrace strenuous intellectual effort. More strongly than almost any other American poet of our century, Stevens has insisted on the value of ideas for poetry. But he has also insisted on the value of intimation, innuendo, and a style based on hints rather than on statement. Never is he strictly literal; for his art he demands a luminosity beyond its intellectual outline: warm, colorful flesh over the intellectual skeleton. This thought is memorably embodied in a poem of twelve lines, "Gallant Château," recalling in its imagery the subtle expression achieved in the culture of Couperin, Watteau, and Racine. Deep aesthetic satisfaction and even deep emotion, the poet believes, may best be conveyed without romantic or melodramatic gestures. Do we wish violent stories and poems whose images include "bitter eyes," "tragic hair," "cold, hostile hands," and violent words, or are we better served by an ordered *mise en scène* and a few words of poetry deftly turned? Stevens affirms his preference for the latter. "Gallant Château" is a most refined statement in behalf of refinement. Stevens' *Collected Poems* is itself such a château.

One of his most brilliant compositions, "Peter Quince at the Clavier," like most of his best works, combines eloquence with intimation, and luminous, rotund statement with an almost shy understatement. The "Quince" in the title, derived from Shakespeare's *A Midsummer Night's Dream*, suggests that the piece is comic rather than tragic and is not to be read in too grave a mood. This is obviously an aesthete's poem, containing a retrospective view of painting, poetry, and music of the baroque period. The word "clavier" in its title would seem to signify harpsichord; the general atmosphere is of a time at least as early as Bach's. The poem could hardly be as it is without recollection of the aesthetic sensibility of that period. Its subject matter belongs to the painters of the seventeenth or even the sixteenth century. Susanna and the elders was, of course, a favorite theme for artists of the times. On the one hand, it had the attractions of the nude, so fascinating a theme for Renaissance and baroque artists; on the other hand, for the orthodox, who revered the Biblical stories and delighted in reflections excited by them. As the great pictorial commentator on the Bible, Rembrandt comes first to mind among those who retailed Susanna's story, and Tintoretto is hardly less conspicuous. This subject and others like it also pleased the older poets and dramatists. George Peele's song opening his play, *David and Bethsabe*, likewise celebrates the seductive charms of a Biblical heroine at her bath and with a delicacy of rhythm and phrase strikingly close to Stevens' poem. The riches of "Peter Quince at the Clavier," when its reflections of music and painting are considered, can hardly be exaggerated. Imagination on the printed page rivals the amplitude of drama. There is a glittering sequence of images and a large and harmoniously contrived series of allusions to sounds: cymbals, horns, tambourines, sighs, simperings, and other noises.

This poem is an Oriental refinement of sensuality, rather in the overtly amorous manner of Persian and Arabic poetry than in the religiously inspired sensuality of India and the Far East. Symbolism is complex. The poet-speaker finds himself in a room in which he hears clavier music and gazes at a lady dressed in blue silk, the favorite color of the French rococo. But his mind drifts off to related thoughts and images, which by devious paths not only accord with his amorous mood but intensify and

purify it. These crystallize into a repetition of the story of
the virtuous Susanna and the lascivious elders, a tale plac-
ing the narrator in a mildly ludicrous light. He has evidently been looking longingly at the lady in blue silk. A
scene in the Oriental style follows. Susanna is bathing in
the pool in the patio of the palace. She is alluringly beautiful, as all the scene is beautiful. Musicians are attending
her at her bath. Abruptly the smooth images of beauty are
ruffled and effaced by the appearance of the passionate
old men. There are no further developments in Stevens'
version of the story. The Biblical tale has served its purpose. It has survived for centuries as a legend of beauty
disturbed by passion, or should it be, by an inappropriate
outburst of passion?

Only strophes two and three paint the picture of Queen
Susanna and the libidinous elders, the first devoted to the
serene episode of the bath, the second, to the ruffled episode of the prying elders detected by the disturbed queen.
Or perhaps the fault was that the elders permitted themselves to be detected? Strophe one gives the poem its general setting, the framing narrative fixing the amorous subject matter in a contemporary time. The fourth, which is
the concluding strophe, indicates that the amorous mood
has at least come under temporary control, reflections on
aesthetics taking its place. The naked has become the
nude, the pure aesthetic attitude at last becoming firmly
established. Social decorum is also sustained. All art, the
poet declares, is sensuous. The piano has its keys, as man
and woman are of flesh and blood. No art or beauty without the material world, not even music, with sound, and
verse, with both sound and imagery. The physical body

dies; from it and its sensibilities springs the body of art, which is immortal. The poet tells us a mystery. The body does not always die but through art becomes deathless, whether it be in the Greek Helen or the Hebraic Susanna. The poem's core is the theme of aesthetic transubstantiation, the world's body lifted to its fruition in art, which is none the less related by cross-influence to the beauty of matter and of the flesh. Nothing is sadder, Stevens declares in "Esthétique du Mal," than the divorce of flesh and spirit. We must at the same time live in the physical world and transcend it through the imagination.

So far as Peter Quince's poem presents a problem to the reader this lies in the detection of the weaving of sound and image in strophes two and three and in the interweaving of the intellectual themes in strophes one and four. The central strophes are a dream projection of the end strophes. Stevens allows nothing to be overclear yet avoids any real obscurantism. It is all logically thought through and entrancingly written, although the images are a little more lush and the thought closer to the beaten track than in most of his finest verse. As a study in suggestion the poem holds a high place; it is an essay on the psychology of eroticism and the psychology of art.

All art, Stevens repeatedly observes, is a species of abstraction. We have noted a number of his poems in which a symbolism from geometry or mathematics is employed, as in his use of angles designated A, B, and C in "So-and-so Reclining on her Couch," or in the title, "The Comedian as the Letter C." Stevens believes equally in sensuous images and abstract conceptions, his poems being both sensuous and intellectual to an uncommon degree. As a student of aesthetics, all kinds of abstraction attract him. Card games, for example, impress him as a discipline akin to art. In "Solitaire Under the Oaks" he finds cards an escape to "pure principles." Moreover, concentration on the unreal world of cards resembles the artist's absorption in his own world. Without consciousness and wholly without self-consciousness, artist and card-player alike "know what to think about." Stevens imagines the card game as played under oak trees. The inference is that nature and human life are involved in the theory of the game, which on psychological analysis proves relevant to aesthetic meditation or creation.

Both idealist and skeptic, Stevens at times celebrates art's eternity and dignity without a shadow of doubt, yet at times—though less often—discovers it in the shade of much dubiety. So in "Montrachet-le-Jardin" we found that in a poem of approximately a hundred lines all but the last three are in the most idealistic and heroic manner, and this is undeniably the impression which the poem makes. The poem might never have ended, if the mood had not been broken. The last three lines are a parting concession of skepticism. Stevens makes it a rule that he shall follow no rule without exception. The narrative "Page from a Tale" makes astonishing reading in his *Collected Poems*. The same can be said of a lurid dream-fantasy, or versified nightmare, "Prologues to What Is Possible." Above all, far from the usual course of his meditations, in "Madame la Fleurie" the sinister cat of which we had a parting glimpse to chill the blood in "Montrachet-le-Jardin" appears again. This poem, written when he was approaching the end of his life, is a dark, macabre speculation, casting a black shadow over his past and his art. Has he in reality, as he fears, been merely dreaming, looking at life only in a mirror, writing under compulsion?

> It was a language he spoke, because he must,
>   yet did not know.
> It was a page he had found in the handbook
>   of heartbreak.

Is the universe in truth as he has depicted it, "a bearded queen, wicked in her dead light"? Is life essentially mad, like a clown in a circus?

The chief difficulty in grasping this poem is largely eliminated when it is read in a far more biographical sense than most of its author's works. Stevens knew that he wrote under a compulsion, that his quest for reality through art was obsessive; in his obsession he detected a streak of the abnormal, much as, according to tradition, Lucretius knew his own compulsion to be tainted with abnormality. The great eloquence of "Madame la Fleurie" can best be accounted for by regarding it as a genuine confession of doubt wrung from its author in a dark hour. It is fortunate for both him and his readers that he experienced few such hours, but fortunate also that undergoing them he made honest use of them in a handful of poems or passages in a sinister mood, reminding us of the much more lurid and less controlled "terrible sonnets" of Gerard Manley Hopkins.

Sometimes on catechizing himself he dismissed the problem with a jest and a shrug of the shoulders, as in the humorous concluding lines of "The Comedian as the Letter C." More often, his mind and spirits rose strongly to his defense. An inveterate self-critic, though not an excessively self-conscious man, he evidently reread his poems with a sharp critical eye. One poem even suggested to him another. This was almost certainly the case in the instance of two works both to be found in *Opus Posthumous*: "On the Way to the Bus" and "As You Leave the Room." In the second poem there is no doubt that the "you" is really the "I," the poet himself speaking.

"On the Way to the Bus" is one of Stevens' typical poems defining a mood and drawing its imagery from nature. Here the mood is a state of euphoria, or well-being. The positive, happy mood is kept well under control; there is no bland observation, in the manner of Browning's Pippa, that "all's well with the world." But well-being is at least given a fresh and scintillating definition. A sense of clarity and happiness sweeps over him as he walks from home to bus on a bright morning with the earth covered with new snow. The world itself seems a perfect work of art. His being throbs with an ecstatic music. He knows this vision to be basically subjective but he knows, too, that it is inextricably bound up with the splendor of a calm winter day after a storm. The casual has become for him the abstract, the eternal; the physical has become spiritual. Although the experience is of a moment on an ordinary morning in Hartford, the poet knows it to be more than journalism, the news of a day that will soon be forgotten. This poem summarizes the ideas defined at greater length in "The Idea of Order at Key West" and "Peter Quince at the Clavier."

"As you Leave the Room" was apparently completed a year after "On the Way to the Bus." Its first eight or nine lines may have been written as early as 1947, according to the conjecture of Samuel French Morse, editor of *Opus Posthumous*. But the last seven lines appear to refer specifically to "On the Way to the Bus." Stevens has again been calling his life as poet to account and wondering if it has not all been misspent in pursuit of an illusion. Or has his fondness for introducing the intellect into poetry reduced his work to the dryness of a skeleton? Are his poems merely the skeletons of poems, not true, living organisms of verse? At this point he recalls a few of his resilient pieces, throbbing with feeling, alive in flesh and blood. He remembers his sensuous "Credences of Summer," with its affirmation of fulfillment in all phases of experience, his poem on the hero, and similar pieces. Above all, he recalls "On the Way to the Bus," celebrating the illumination which he experienced on a winter morning only a few months before, and the resilient faith in life, emotion, and clarity of thought there expressed. No, he concludes, neither he as a man nor his poems are failures, skeletons, the shadows or apologies for life. They are vital, residing at life's core.

IX : *Psychological Insights*

S TEVENS occupied himself with many problems, some unmistakably related to his favorite theme, the aesthetic
experience, others not related to it at all. It may be surprising to some of his readers that a large number of his
poems, possibly not the best, but close to them, concern
themselves with insights into subjects of a more general
psychological interest. This chapter deals with representative poems whose commanding interest lies within such
areas.

Doubtless aesthetic considerations stand in the background of a number of these pieces but they are never conspicuous. This is exemplified by the eloquent poem "The
World as Meditation," which deals with the abstract idea
of obsession. Stevens knew his own obsession, a compul-
sive drive toward the study of the principles of poetry in
relation to the experience of reality. Although this outlook
presumably lies in the background of the poem just mentioned, it never becomes explicit. In literal terms, the
poem's subject is the almost excessive devotion, virtually
a fixation, of Penelope to the absent Ulysses. Her husband

visits her in her dreams. Toward dawn she imagines that she sees him and so vivid is her illusion that she remains long uncertain whether the form that confronts her is apparition or reality. Can her imagination be so strong as to conjure up such a literally faithful image of reality? Thus far this is a love poem, an unresolved study of reality and illusion.

But Stevens is forever bent on symbolism, on overtones, and an effort to reach toward the broadest possible abstractions. Before the poem itself he quotes a few sentences by the celebrated violinist, Georges Enesco, to the effect that, while he has traveled and played his instrument assiduously, he has been continually haunted by the daemon of composition, which has flourished upon private meditation. This has been his ruling passion. The idea clearly attracted Stevens. It is curious that his lifelong involvement with the conception of a ruling passion should have so nearly approached one of the views of Alexander Pope, a poet with whom he shared so much, although the differences between the Augustan and the modern are conspicuously great. One of these differences is Stevens' more persistent fear that this passion may be also illusion, that a dominant faith may be wholly subjective and wholly false. His poem is a proposition applicable to almost any great love or devotion. How shall the haunting power be appraised? Illusion or not, it commonly constitutes an essentially barbarous because uncivilized force. Also, true or false, it may afford an incentive to live and to live heroically. The epic, or heroic, background of "The World as Meditation" must not be overlooked. If the individual believes in his own compulsion, he stands at least part way on the road to dignity and happiness. The poem opens lines of thought unexplored within itself, yet its thought is better described as fundamental in Stevens' world of speculations than as incidental. The poem proves to be an eloquent and impressive work.

Fastidious in definition, Stevens is clearly loath to dogmatize regarding reality and illusion and similarly hesitates to define the distinction between the complete and fully understood experience and that which is incomplete and only partially grasped. So much in life and art he finds half known, half unknown, in one respect fulfilled and satisfying, in another unfulfilled and tantalizing. As Shelley declared, in our greatest happiness lies a hidden want. The stunted vision commonly accompanies the satisfied heart. The thinker or artist is torn apart, the sight being gratified, the mind never gratified. As Stevens observes in the final line of one of his most accomplished poems, "The Well Dressed Man with a Beard," "It can never be satisfied, the mind, never."

"How Now, O, Brightener . . ." deals with this problem. The conclusion is suspended in pure irony. The brightest and most joyous experiences are, perhaps, the least definable. Something of a continuous frustration haunts the mind. Spring, for instance, cannot be captured in thought. At that most entrancing season of the year the sun sparkles most elusively, there is a green edged with yellow and a blue edged with green that especially delight the eye but trouble the mind. All natural blessings are too complex for thought, simple love being the most complex of all. Life abounds in illusions and dewy favors, while our wills remain stunted beyond redemption. "How Now, O, Brightener . . ." illustrates these ideas with a highly sensitive parable in verse altogether typical of its author's most mature style, and accordingly it well repays careful pondering.

Although Stevens is far from being an antirationalist—is, in fact, an ardent believer in ideas—he entertains no illusions as to the precision of either philosophical or poetic thought. On some occasions his thinking is clouded and wintry, oppressed with awareness of the inadequacy of thought. The position is stated in the oft-quoted words from the last section of "Owl's Clover":

> We have grown weary of the man that thinks.
> He thinks and it is not true.

Much of Stevens' sad wisdom reminds the reader of the book of Ecclesiastes, for his aphorisms and several of his shorter poems tend to a distinctly philosophical melancholy. "The Region November," first published in 1956, describes this melancholy state. The poem's imagery proves uncommonly simple, familiar, and direct. The north wind of November swaying the treetops conjures in his mind the thought of the soul pondering "God, the world and human nature, pensive on the waste throne of its own wilderness." For all its grandeur, thought sways back and forth with the windy aimlessness of the November treetops. Yet even here is no blank pessimism. The wind, after all, has its grave beauty, and it is the highest branches that sway most, the hero and the noblest of mankind being those who feel most keenly the gusts blowing out of the chill of infinity.

A similar thought occurs in a much earlier poem and one frequently cited, "The Curtains in the House of the Metaphysician." This is a more personal work than the foregoing, neither quite satire nor quite self-congratulation. Stevens notes the ponderous, cloudlike undulations of the curtains in the metaphysician's study, connoting silence, solitude, and the vast motions of the stars and firmament. Here is "The last largeness, bold to see." This line, the conclusion of the piece, is decidedly affirmative and heroic. Yet in its general tone the poem weighs heavily with melancholy; and, after all, it seems no great compliment to the thinker to associate his meditations with the mysterious, ponderous swaying of dark curtains, behind which even a raven might be lurking. A sad, deep irony casts its long shadow across this extremely fine and moving work. It, too, must be long pondered before it yields its full flavor. Many readers have almost certainly regarded it as more smart than profound. Why write a poem about a curtain and why hang a philosopher's study with such unlikely drapery? What can be concealed behind it? Reflection, however, dispels such strictures, showing that in these instances the shallowness or superficiality, so far as it exists, is with the imperceptive and hasty reader, not with the poet's calculating hand and mind.

Some of his pages are exceedingly shrewd in exploring psychological problems or, in other words, in describing the nature of our thought and experience. Brevity and an apparent casualness often tend to conceal his real insight. Such is the case with a poem of sonnet length, "Man Carrying Thing." The artfully chosen title faithfully indicates the skill with which Stevens deals with abstractions. The poem is provided with a sudden turn of the wrist at its conclusion. The body of the piece gives an accurate description of two items both blurred in the twilight beyond clear recognition. One is a man whose identity cannot be discerned, the other a bundle which he carries and which remains mysterious in the gathering darkness. We know that we see a man and that he is carrying a bundle. This is primary. Secondary things we do not know. We must wait, the last sentence declares, until dawn, when "the bright obvious stands motionless in cold." There is an air of precision and fastidiousness about the poem, revealing a mind sharpened to a fine integrity. Only a thoughtful person would explore such apparently obvious elements. Yet the basic thought is not obvious, at least in the poem itself. Stevens distinguishes between abstraction and concretion, between significant and moving generality on the one hand and the less significant and less moving specific incident on the other. Dawn is cold and bright but motionless and virtually dead. With dawn, poetry gives way to prose.

Stevens' unusual insight extends also into the region of personality and the emotions of the psyche most conspicuously treated by the novelists, those writers whose peculiar outlook was first disclosed along with the refinement of letter writing in the early years of the eighteenth century. This is clearly not Stevens' preferred field, any more than drama proved congenial to him, and in each case his limitations spring from a common source. Yet the powers of poetic imagination are never rigidly restricted by literary genres or categories and a number of distinguished poems in something of the manner of the psychological novelists materially widen the scope of Stevens' work. "Two Letters" serves as a good illustration. These delicately felt and rather elusive poems disclose many of his favorite insights into the personal life. The relationship which he views most fondly lies in a somewhat uncommon region midway between the familiar conceptions of love and friendship.

His world may at first seem cold, but this is largely an illusion. It is not without erotic passion; a glow and fire lies within much of his poetry that may not at once be obvious but will be strongly felt as the thoughtful reader stands for any length of time in close proximity to it. Similarly, his undeniable austerity and reticence, equally that of the cultured New Englander and of the fastidious artist, by no means renders him essentially unsocial. Of his social insights more will be said later. Nothing morose can be detected in his conception of the personal or emotional life. Though the poetry is certainly not warmed with the romantic glow of a gregarious mood, as is Whitman's or Sandburg's or even Frost's, in all of whom one discovers a genial disposition to embrace mankind the impulse to friendship is far from absent.

With Stevens, the popular, romantic conception of amorous or friendly relationships is lacking, but not sensuous warmth and not emotional involvement. He places his highest valuation here on intuitive emotional understanding, on a relationship not conspicuously related to either sex or the intellect but established on the impulse to nearness and to extreme confidence, interdependence, and irresistible affection. Among his favorite signs or symbols of affection are silence and secrecy. Friendship may not be loosely shared nor broadly communicated. It exists between two people, or between three, or within an entire family. It may be projected imaginatively by poet or novelist but not in itself spread promiscuously about nor extended into the indiscriminate love of mankind frequently announced as the goal of religious idealism. The Buddha of meditation is well known to Stevens but not the Buddha of universal love. His outlook would recognize a distinction between Jesus' love for his disciples and his comprehensive affection for mankind.

The remarkable little poem "A Woman Sings a Song for a Soldier Come Home," which will be examined in some detail in a later chapter, when the emotional values of his verse are discussed, must be cited here as a preliminary to the analysis of his view of personal feeling. In this case, as in several others, he uses the image of a secret meeting outside the limits of a town, where lovers meet in a field or wood protected from the gaze of the many. The image is in part sexual but is also more than that. It helps in the definition of his view of intimacy as the root-meaning of affectionate social relationships. "Two Letters" affords his most refined and precise statement of his insight in this regard.

The two poems, imagined as letters written by two persons, are virtually one in the sense that their full power cannot be felt if they are read without relation to each other. One refers to "love," the other specifically rejects the designation of the relationship as love. The core of the thought is the vast satisfaction felt in a relationship of mutual affection. By uniting in friendship, two persons, whose sex is deliberately unspecified, experience a profound gratification, an awareness that they have entered into a new world resembling an ineffably congenial landscape. Not even the most glorious sights of nature or the most genial conditions in general social life quite equal this ease, this intimate, most happy intercourse, founded upon the heart, in no sense upon the mind.

The letters are of fifteen and twelve lines respectively. The six concluding lines of the first letter rather curiously but most significantly describe not a relationship between two persons but the spirit prevading a small company of persons, perhaps a family, possibly a group of friends. These persons are depicted in the intimacy of candlelight, exchanging words that the hearers wish intensely to hear, hanging on each other's speech as the listener hangs on the revelations of a story, and bound together with complete mutual confidence and belief. In its physical proportions the scene is small and intimate; in its spiritual proportions, vast or even infinite. Such friendship comprehends all the best qualities of works of poetry and art, unobtrusive, compressed, emotional, completely gratifying. The poem's images are exquisitely conceived. The second letter continues the thought of the first, stressing, however, the epistolary idea. Most noteworthy of all in the many remarkable qualities of friendship as described here is that it transcends time and place, in which it conspicuously differs from sex. Letters between friends define their relation even more fully than their meeting. For friendship's circle remains unbroken by distance of any kind; it remains circular and complete despite "the miles of distance away." "Two Letters," though completely without the glamorous rhetoric of Stevens' early work, is, in fact, one of his most rewarding achievements in artistic form and emotional awareness.

Clearly, the foregoing poem is of idealism all compact. But Stevens knows the "real" world too well to limit his poetic vision to idealism, either tender or heroic. He tastes the world with salt and vinegar as well. In other words, his view of human psychology includes profuse ingredients of irony and satire. In illustration of this are two poems rendered at least a little difficult, not, as "Two Letters," because of heightened spiritual sensibility, but because of acute observations of the manners and moods of historical man. The two are alike in dealing with decadent sophistication in the aesthetic life, one glancing at British aestheticism of the last generation, the other at French, or possibly cosmopolitan, aestheticism of the present generation. Both are, as refined satire should be, sly, witty, and rich in intimation—in fact, less representative of satire as generally understood than of high comedy with a wry turn toward the macabre.

The title "Anglais Mort à Florence" contains in relation to the poem designated the appropriately Dantesque irony concerning persons physically alive but spiritually or essentially dead. Nothing in Stevens' poem indicates that the Englishman in question is literally dead. Quite the contrary, he is living in a vacuum of mind and futility of soul broadly similar to that of T. S. Eliot's Prufrock. His error has been to love music sentimentally, to develop the personality of the parasitic aesthete, passive and not impossibly homosexual. With much insight into the spirit of the last century, Stevens describes his victim as a lover of Brahms. The unfortunate man suffers the last dilapidation of a spirit that has always been weak. As a young man he had exhibited at least enough independence to stand alone, or so it seems to him in retrospect. Later he gave himself in a passive, sentimental servitude to Brahms. Obviously he was the sycophantic aesthete, neither musicologist, critic, nor performer. His acquaintance with music is not knowledge but vague emotion, not a grasp of structure, technique, or content, but only of certain vague overtones of feeling within a rigidly subjective consciousness. The art to which he has, ironically, been sincerely and passionately devoted he has never understood.

Somehow in ways unspecified, Brahms, though himself sufficiently alive, composed a type of music on which aesthetes of this nature fasten for their insipid nutriment —barnacles on the ship of art. Perhaps Brahms himself represents the last, declining phase of a musical tradition, with a romantic involvement in emotionalism in music contrary to the severe aesthetic of the vastly more robust J. S. Bach. The poem, however, is wisely focused not on the complex problem of Brahms but on the relatively simple problem of the imaginary English gentleman of leisure, the expatriate in Florence.

At the end of his train of errors this man finds himself spiritually desiccated. Even Brahms no longer gives him real pleasure. The mere puppet of respectable, bourgeois convention, he finds that he stands alone by virtue "of God's help and the police;" not a valid human being but a puppet of a speciously pious church and a paternal state, not an authentic man but a mere engraving of conventional respectability. In twenty-eight lines Stevens achieves a portrait that Browning, with all his skill, might have labored through twenty-eight pages to a less pointed result.

The type of mind depicted in "Anglais Mort à Florence," with its title suggesting a minor notice in a French social newspaper, belongs to a generation or age now largely passed. Perhaps when Stevens wrote it he had read Thorstein Veblen's *Theory of the Leisure Class*. In depicting his Englishman, Stevens is more or less at ease, supercilious, humorous, and relaxed. The type of mind delineated in "The Novel," on the contrary, belongs to our own generation and is treated by Stevens more satirically, without the geniality invited by the perspective of history. Here Brahms is replaced by Camus. The novelist is treated more sympathetically than the musician, the aesthete more caustically. In the former case, Brahms became a symbol for lush emotional romanticism, with its sentimentality, spurious optimism, or complacency; in the latter, Camus provides a symbol for bitter intellectual disillusionment, with its exaggerated and self-conscious pessimism. Yet in neither case is the criticism leveled primarily at the artist, either musician or novelist. The onus falls on the parasite, or passive follower, who distorts the meaning of his master or possibly also exaggerates the faults or weaknesses actually found in the master. Basically the chief defect in both the Englishman of the first poem and the Spaniard of the second is a lack of personal strength, a dependence upon tradition—one man, as we now see it, upon the thought of the old guard, the other upon that of the avant-garde. Each is an example of the inglorious position of camp follower. Each breathes a vapor upon the too closely inspected mirror reflecting his times. That each looks not at life but at art's mirror of life, and so misjudges art itself, is the meaning of the trenchant mirror image in "The Novel."

As one misjudged music, the other misjudged poetry. The young Spanish-speaking intellectual, chilly in his rented room in Paris, has come from a land in which poetry has been to him a sonorous incantation, a wine going to the head, curbing thought, inflating the ego, never truly stimulating the individual and his imaginative life. The young man is essentially shallow, capable of no emotion except despair. Under the guidance of cosmopolitan thought in Paris he has accumulated many ideas, none of which is properly his own. His mind is a parody of the critical intellect, for his intellectuality is as spurious and borrowed as his aesthetic sensibility. Like the Englishman of the last century, he is sterile and parasitic, in his case not fastened on the traditions of neoclassical art in Italy or neoclassical music in Germany (each tradition essentially romantic) but on the "futilitarianism" of the age of *The Waste Land*. The poem is Stevens' rebuke of the Grub Street of his own day, from which he himself stood so severely aloof and which in historical perspective he found grubbier than ever. The verse-portrait, a typical character sketch combining the best insights of such art from Theophrastus to Camus, is of high value. Although general aesthetic theory and keen literary criticism stand in the poem's background, it is essentially a social study and critique of his own times, informed with an exceptional acuteness in psychological observation. It can hardly be too long or too carefully examined, for every image is calculated, even though a genuine spontaneity enlivens the whole.

X : *Phases of Emotion*

To ANALYZE the heart, as Stevens does in such poems as
we have just examined, it is necessary to know it.
Emotion is indubitably expressed in these poems on the
vicissitudes of the psyche, but in these the psychological
insight of an intellectual or intuitive nature seems even
more noteworthy than the direct expression of feeling.
Passionate experience in them, as in many others of
Stevens' poems, is held conspicuously aloof. As already observed, a widely received view of his works conceives them
as cold and replete with artifice, witty, intellectual, fastidi-
ously composed, works of extreme formalism, by no means
springing from deep feeling or expressing such experience.
Such an opinion distorts the picture. As a rule reticent,
according to the New England tradition or the Anglo-
Saxon Protestant tradition in general, many of Stevens'
poems arise from intense feelings and convey them to the
discerning reader. In these cases it would be amiss to describe the emotion itself as repressed; under the rigid control of art, it is nevertheless a force of alarming power. His
poems may have a smooth, cool surface, but so does the

snow before an avalanche. Intense passion is the theme of any number of his pieces, which might, to borrow his own terms, be called postcards from a volcano. The heart is farsighted, discerning best from a certain distance.

An interpretive analysis of such poems is useful because it refutes the view of him as remote or Olympian and because, their intensity notwithstanding, even these pieces invariably present at least some difficulties to the reader. Although possessing the emotional force which he is accustomed to find in romantic writing or in any strongly moving verse, they are still likely to be rich in intimations, overtones, symbolic expressions, and a profuse metaphorical style. Rarely, if ever, in these pieces do we find a direct or simple expression pervading the whole, as in a typical poem by Burns. It is true that in almost every poem a few phrases will be strikingly or even shockingly unadorned, naked, and without a trace of rhetoric. Such style is a stop which Stevens pulls out on his organ when the moment in his art demands it. But as a rule he reconciles elegance and subtlety of expression with even the most volcanic of emotional material. It is of some moment that the poems now in question repay careful analysis hardly less than those of a more distinctly witty or intellectual character.

In dealing with the storms and upheavals of the heart Stevens was in possession of both the theory and the reality; he had an explanation of and an apology for the emotions and an experience of their force coursing alarmingly through his blood and soul. His intellectual view of the passionate phase of life becomes one of the themes in his best-known poem, "Sunday Morning." This poem is an apology for the most ardent feelings as a normal and gratifying part of the adventure of living. It is couched as a defense of a survival of primitive or elemental forces even in the most sophisticated and highly developed civilization. The symbol of Sunday is chosen as a dramatic crossroads between traditions of urbane civilization and those of vehement religious experience. From one point of view the holiday marks the most favorable opportunity for a leisured class in a mature or even decadent society to regale itself; from another, it signifies an occasion for release of the most vehement religious excitement. Both culture and religion postulate a good or even perfect life, here termed "paradise," a life of uncontaminated happiness. An overrefined culture imagines such happiness virtually within its grasp, only to find that happiness eludes it. Frigidity and ennui attend the life without vigorous and natural feeling. Men cannot live contented without emotional commitments. Neither can they be content without the exercises of the emotional life which earlier cultures experienced through religion and which later cultures must experience through channels of expression combining religious fervor with the excitations of a deeply moving art.

The poet selects the modern, urban woman, surrounded with every luxury and endowed with the finest sensibility and cultivation, as representative of the sophisticated life. Yet in her greatest luxury and ease she experiences "a hidden want." Her thoughts instinctively drift back to the turbulent story of the Christian religion. As the poet ponders the scene, he recalls earlier ages when the mythologies of the world's religions conferred their riches on both the emotional and the imaginative life. To a certain degree the problems broached by this poem stand beside those posed by so many other of Stevens' works, namely, the problems of the world of art. The oversophisticated woman finds emptiness in her heart because of a want of emotional conviction, and her art pale and merely decorative from the same cause. Serious art, Stevens observes, shares much with religious experience, and though the faith of the ancients cannot be retained in our advanced rationalistic civilization, something of the spiritual and emotional energy of the older world must be maintained if our culture is not to be dissipated by spiritual malaise and a comprehensive ennui.

Stevens contrasts the illusion of perfect happiness with both the realities of life and the turbulence of the ancient myths. Complete and unbroken contentment has been in early religions merely a hypothesis, never a serious assumption. Experience proves it invalid even in the most sophisticated and privileged society. There is no valid aristocracy of professional pleasure seekers. Life is not complete with the comic philosophy alone. (Stevens' position in this regard should give pause to any critic who holds that his philosophy is the comic view only.) Life, he asserts, is tragedy and demands the tragic outlook. The view expressed in "Sunday Morning" is clearly eclectic. Necessary experiences and insights lie with both the dramatically conflicting parties, with the modern sophisticated woman who here supplies the secondary theme, and with the primitive celebrants who supply the primary theme. In its balanced outlook the poem seems eminently classical, an orientation with which the formal rhetoric and rigid stanzaic structure admirably accord. "Sunday Morning" becomes a hymn, or ode, to the full or complete life.

A philosophy of death affords an important key to the

poem's meaning, as the theme of death provides a leading element in its ordering. To deny death is to deny vitality. The woman who begins her meditations with the utmost complacence finds herself presently faced with the eternal realities of decay and extinction. From one point of view the poem is a counterpart to the high comedy of "Prufrock," and "Le Monocle de Mon Oncle." The pretensions of those who fancy themselves resisting time's indignities are in Eliot's poem exposed to ridicule with a disturbing melancholy, in Stevens' with a more explicitly comic and healthy vision. Those poems are inspired by a wry or dry comedy. "Sunday Morning," on the contrary, is conceived in the temper of high tragedy. The woman escapes from depression and frustration by immersion in an eminently serious and almost primitive mode of experience. Although it is not explicitly said that she feels her age creeping upon her and possibly on those she loves, the poem intimates this far more impressively than would be the case had the statement been made directly. On looking about her she observes decay and death. Later she sees also resurrection and life, for the basic fact of life on earth, unlike life in a hypothetical "paradise," is simply that it is forever perishing and renewing itself. As Stevens with great skill weaves his themes, much as themes are interwoven in music, there is no spring without fall, no summer without winter, no joy without pain, no life without death. The realist accepts this fact. He establishes himself in a world forever experiencing these transitions, this divine tragedy and divine comedy. He must even come to love the sad declensions of a real autumn more truly than the dream of an imaginary paradise in heaven or the no less vain dream of a paradise on earth. There is no paradise in nature, only the pause and fulfillment of summer slipping shortly into fall. But meditation can make even the violence of winter seem gentle, for it is a part of the scheme denying to the wise man either complete ecstasy or despair. The poem ends exquisitely upon a note of quiet reconciliation.

Before the final stanza comes one that asserts the undying claims of a virtually primitive emotional violence. Stevens is clearly thinking in accord with the best insights of his age. It would be remiss to read this important poem without some thought also of the neoprimitive in the music of Stravinsky's *Sacre de Printemps,* or *Les Noces,* or the neoprimitivism of "The Women of Arles," and other works by Picasso and his associates in art. Stevens was simply writing in the more adventurous spirit of his times. From the standpoint of literary history, his poem is a blast against the low emotional tone and spiritual debility of the Georgian poets. It was written contemporaneously with the best of Expressionist writing in Germany, with the prose of D. H. Lawrence, and with Hart Crane's *The Bridge,* in which poem primitive ritual also plays a conspicuous role.

"Sunday Morning" is possibly marred by the lushness of its rhetoric. In it are several instances of a "poetic" diction that now seems outmoded; the essentially classical form, though according well with much of the eclectic philosophy, may not harmonize so well with the turbulent, neoprimitive imagery. Presumably such a poem as "Esthétique du Mal" is more mature art. But the profuse decorations of spring will always be as much admired as the austerities of winter, and "Sunday Morning" be regarded as a wise and eminently comely masterpiece. More than a critique of the emotions, it expresses them; if at times the expression comes through a veil of rhetoric more appropriate in the comic "Le Monocle de Mon Oncle," few readers will deny that for a singularly reflective and abstract poem, "Sunday Morning" is deeply moving.

The elegance of innumerable phrases in "Sunday Morning" induces an admiration for the style over and above an understanding of the whole. The sum of the parts must often have been enjoyed less than the parts themselves. Stevens himself seems to have been aware of a problem here, for he did considerable rearranging of the poem when it was published for the second time. There is a tendency for the individual stanzas to stand too much apart, as though a sequence of sonnets and not a completely unified poem were intended. Stevens never relinquished a fondness for this episodic construction, even when writing the last of his longer poems. Obviously a slow and fastidious workman, he thought much in terms of stanzas, perhaps influenced by the strophic structure of Greek choral odes. His besetting tendency was always toward intricacy, so that his long poems become at times overwritten and overinvolved, and it is this outcome which renders his shorter pieces, with only a few important exceptions, on the whole not only more attractive but more admirable. The basic ideas of "Sunday Morning" he expressed in other works less eloquent but at least more trenchant. An instance would be the first poem in his volume *Parts of a World*, the high-spirited "Parochial Theme." Yet even this poem is not without some complexity. In its philosophy, it is "Sunday Morning" in reverse.

It begins where "Sunday Morning" left off, with a celebration of the "archaic," or primitive, and concludes with a declaration of the inadequacy of this outlook to meet the full demands of the modern world. By the "archaic," a word several times repeated as a formal term in Stevens' philosophy, is signified an essentially unphilosophical attitude toward life, a naïve view raising no doubts and recognizing no problems. Young and confident athletes might share it. According to this outlook, life is heroic, virile, intense, emotional, spontaneously experienced and expressed, wholly unsentimental, and possibly sublime. The archaic age is the heroic or epic age, standing in sharp contrast with our own—though youthful America has sometimes appeared almost as a parody of it. Stevens' thinking here has its roots as far back as German speculation in the times of Lessing, Goethe, and Schiller. In "Sunday Morning" he asserts modern civilization's need to retain some contact with the primitive. In "Parochial Theme" he comments on the idea further by asserting its inadequacy as an answer or solution to the issues of modern life.

Simple joy in the physical world and in physical exertion and excitement is brilliantly expressed in the first half of "Parochial Theme." This part of the poem suggests a number of Stevens' other lusty lyrics, notably the first poem in his first volume, "Earthy Anecdote" in *Harmonium*. Again, the imagery includes animals. Here they are ponies ridden briskly through autumn woods. The riders are Parisians, seeking relaxation and escape from unpleasant problems too insistent to be denied. They are the irresponsibles. Over this poem, as over many of the pages of *Parts of a World*, hovers the shadow of war and its brother, death. Without prosaic explanations that could only have proved superfluous, Stevens abruptly reflects that within a year the bones of riders and horses may strew the very hills on which they have exercised so joyfully. All this bright color and ecstasy, so vividly suggesting youth, will come to nought. The ardent young materialists must discover to their grief that they have thought too superficially to protect their own happiness. This happiness has been only a squandering of youthful brilliance and energy. In his last line the poet issues a warning too cogent in its essence and too colloquial in its diction to appear in the least didactic: "Piece the world together, boys, but not with your hands." Stevens warns against the reckless pursuit of even the most robust pleasures. The lusty young men, hard riders of horses, are as much or more to blame for the predicament of modern society as the relaxed and supersophisticated women depicted in "Sunday Morning." Sport is war in infancy; maturity signifies a meditative and a reflective life.

The poem is in a sense a critique of much of the mood and subject matter of modern art. Just as one can hardly read "Sunday Morning" without thinking of Picasso and Stravinsky, so one can hardly read "Parochial Theme" without thinking of the miraculously skilfull drawings of race horses by Dégas, Manet, and Lautrec. Clearly, Stevens enjoys such subjects in art, just as, with absolute frankness and honesty, he praises physical joys. But these he finds not enough. The entire materialistic philosophy which they represent to him in his eyes seems tragically inadequate. "Parochial Theme," the initial poem in *Parts of a World*, becomes an apology for the more involved poems to follow in that and other of his volumes. An expression of a gusty emotion, "Parochial Theme" must be held one of the lustiest poems in American literature.

That the urgency of sex, the most violent of the emotions, plays a less conspicuous role in Stevens' poetry than in the work of the larger number of poets, novelists, and playwrights by no means signifies its absence. His manner of writing verse simply means that these emotions are expressed more obliquely than usual: the violence is present but under unusually strict control. "Last Look at Lilacs" offers a good example of his approach. Here, as in many of his poems, written both early and late in his career, the tepid, timid lover is ridiculed, the robust and insistent lover portrayed in a flattering light. In such matters Stevens is obviously a realist, though he looks also with much favor on the conscious artifices of courtship. "Last Look at Lilacs" contrasts two types of lovers. The first dilates on the features of an entrancing landscape in the manner of a chemist or a botanist, neglecting to note that the girl at his side experiences nature altogether differently, that she is emotionally stimulated by the spring blossoms and fully prepared to welcome his most earnest advances. An evening star shines brightly upon them, the augury of the advancing season and the robust Don Juan, "well booted, rugged, arrogantly male . . . who will embrace her before summer comes." The scene is set in an "Hymeneal air." The lukewarm lover fails to "Feel her body quivering in the Floreal." This is a poetry with strong penetration into the essence of sex, totally without the banal eroticism encountered in less imaginative writers. The forces behind passion are strongly felt; their physical manifestations not prosaically recounted but imaginatively intimated. "Last Look at Lilacs" is a highly competent poem of love. Stevens captures the fragrance of the emotion without the decadent animalism so popular in the avant-garde of the nineteen-twenties, when this aristocratic poem was written.

Far from being pale and overintellectual after the bespectacled manner of the large genus of American poets essentially academic, Stevens' poetry contains draughts of the very deepest gusto. Strong winds blow through it; hot sunlight shines upon it. Sap fairly bursts its limbs. Some of this strength in sensuous imagination appears to be owing to the French tradition, of which this thoughtful and most cosmopolitan New Englander was an enthusiastic scholar. T. S. Eliot studied a few of the least representative Frenchmen while Stevens studied the French tradition as a whole. He owes much to the French painters from Renoir to Matisse and much, also, to the French masters of the nude in the painting and sculpture of the baroque period. In this regard he appreciates the ancestry of the modern style. As he writes in "St. Armorer's Church from the Outside:" "It is like a new account of everything old." This poem describes a church dramatically divided into two halves. One half is a ruin which, however, nature has reclaimed with some beauty of its own. The ruin spells decadence and an ascetic melancholy. A small chapel, on the contrary, is decorated with paintings described as even gayer than those by Matisse at Vence. These pictures express the joy of life in all its sensuous power. As always, the robust Stevens rises to rare heights in celebrating this theme. Here is writing of extreme virtuosity, dazzlingly fresh, disturbingly emotional. The chapel is described as a land "of ruddy-ruby fruits," with an air "of freshness, clearness, greenness, blueness." It is suited to its age but also to the newest inventions of the age, like "the first car out of a tunnel." This is both emotional and high-spirited—a style with an immense verve.

Something of the same hard gusto and racy flavor is found in a slighter poem with a more occasional outlook, "The Drum-Majors in the Labor Day Parade." This slashing trifle appeared in the little magazine *Smoke* in 1934, during the dark period of the great American economic depression. But if it is political at all, it is so only in its taunting, ironic castigation of the weak leadership and want of vigor in American labor. Actually, its subject is neither political nor economic. With much verve and brio, the poem deplores the want of such qualities among the laborers nominally celebrating their historic triumphs. Although it was never republished in Stevens' lifetime, as typical of one aspect of his mind and his emotional vitality it repays consideration. Hardly difficult to grasp, it appears somewhat surprisingly in *Opus Posthumous* among many far more sober compositions. If not for its singular vitality and the dynamite of its taunting irony, it might be described as light verse. A more vigorous specimen of satire would be hard to find in twentieth-century American poetry. With its peculiar stanza, two short rhyming lines followed by a still shorter whiplash of an unrhymed line, as if in scorn of the preceding couplet, the words fairly crash along like a cataract. They are insulting and so intended. Italians are rudely called "Dagoes." The marchers are described as "mechanical bears," as possibly the mere toys of their millionaire employers. The two concluding stanzas, where the rhymes are omitted, admirably typify Stevens' high spirits, the tang on his tongue, his uproarious humor and zest for living:

> They ought to be muscular men,
> Naked and stamping the earth,
> Whipping the air.
> The banners should brighten the sun.
> The women should sing as they march.
> Let's go home.

The sheer energy, vigor, and drive of this approaches Swift at his best. It is a side of Stevens as yet too little regarded. He himself neglected to republish this piece in any of his volumes.

Much of his emotional energy is in his satirical poems, where we encounter some hate but more malice. Behind his dry humor there clearly lies a mind packed with explosives all the more dangerous on this account. Outbursts of fiery feeling come unexpectedly, like flashes of summer lightning. So *Harmonium* contains a short poem, "Some Friends from Pascagoula," which unexpectedly hurls a Jovian thunderbolt. Perhaps as much might be inferred from the sinister place-name with which the good-humored title ends. Stevens takes pleasure in a savagery that he discovers in both the Negroes and the land in which he finds them. He feels that only a Negro could best describe the fierce descent of an eagle on its prey. The lines depict "the sun-bronzed air," the intense glare of light on sand and trees, the plunge of the great bird, less heroic but no less fiery and fatal than Pindar's eagle. A deep thirst for strong emotion impels the words. From the lips of a black and sly Negro the poet longs to hear the epic description. The last line, like the fast lens of a camera, catches the eagle's final dive: "Speak of the dazzling wings." Nothing could be more virile or farther from the insipidities of Georgian verse.

With powerful feelings Stevens traces the malice of events. In "No Possum, No Sop, No Taters" he again nerves his verses with a working-class temper. This poem appears in *Parts of a World* along with many other bitterly felt reflections on the world of war and economic injustice. Here it is not the fury of the tropic sun but the devastation of frost-bound winter that inspires him. Conditions are bad for the farmer. In fact, they could hardly be worse. Yet with a vast resilience he declares that there is exhilaration in having struck bottom, in having reached the worst. Times are hostile and challenging. But their very malice evokes desperate resistance. With these thoughts the poem might end. Stevens, however, gives, as usual, a final twist. As a crow rises from the blasted earth, the poet notices "the malice in his eye." The sinister glint comes not only from the crow's eye, it proceeds from the poet's spirit. Intensity of feeling lies behind the lines, all the stronger since the words expressing it are severely reticent and rigorously pressed down.

Sometimes this emotional awareness of the Spirit Sinister appears to Stevens to spread over almost all surfaces of life. The wing of Calvinism harshly brushes his pen; the malice becomes diabolic. Such is the case in two poems, interestingly enough, like the two just discussed, enforced with imagery from birds. "Domination of Black" is one of its author's most lyrical and symbolic works, a dance of words with dark intent spreading metaphysical wings. The imagery is something of a *tour de force*, the lines plotted almost too consciously, the whole a bit too choreographic—with the probable exception of the last eight lines, a calculated climax pulling all parts tightly together. This macabre quartet is a dance of four symbolic figures: the peacocks, the fire, the wind, the hemlocks. The peacocks have the last word, or rather, the last cry. The culminating surprise comes as the poet's vision passes beyond the room and even beyond the windows of the room to rove at least in spirit under the open sky. There shines a malicious star, like a spark from a human hearth, but darkly suggesting that all the starry universe is no other than a fire lit in a funereal darkness, blown to fury by ferocious winds and originating in a source whose voice is the evil shriek of the peacock, that bird so alluring in plumage, so evil within, its cry being a symbol of its malicious heart. The quartet has turned into a quintet. This star is the anti-Christ, the antithesis of the Star of Bethlehem.

Although "Domination of Black" is to an extraordinary degree abstract, it is deeply charged with underground violence. Earthquake and volcanic fire lie beneath the feet of the quaint dancers. Externally, the work is a prodigy of virtuosity; it is also a delicately carved receptacle of the most intense feeling. At heart it has an Oriental subtlety and sophistication, with the condensed fury of Sanskrit mythology. The peacock has its geographical as well as its spiritual significance. Ultimately it is fanatic India that fathered "Domination of Black." Only a deeply emotional being could have composed these tense and almost liturgical lines.

There is, perhaps, less art and less vehemence, but an even clearer expression of sinister and malicious destiny in "The Bird with the Coppery, Keen Claws." Like peacock and phoenix, the bird is a sun symbol. One infers it to be a symbol in a philosophy wherein the sun is no friendly, fructifying agent but a blasting and withering diabolic force. Imagery here is also brilliantly conceived, with an Oriental flavor, as witness the allusion to the "golden alguazil." Hardly since the Persian Attar and his *Bird Parliament* have birds been grasped with such symbolic value as in Stevens' poetry. By various devices he conveys, if his reader is at least passably competent, the metaphysical or abstract meaning of his poem. With this meaning is also involved the sense of irony and paradox. The bird is "a parakeet of parakeets;" grotesque, immense; at once moving and not moving; his tails deploy "panache upon panache;" his terrible claws as yet remain immovable. He is blind because, in the sinister veiw, the physical universe is blind. Though physically small, to the imagination he is malicious and vast: "His tip a drop of water full of storms." This metaphysical poetry has great intensity. A drop from Stevens' pen contains a hurricane.

Fortunately for the development of a manner or style charged with great feeling, he by no means allows the abstract or the metaphysical to dominate his pages. He is, as he professes to be, a modern humanist, a new humanist, though certainly not a member of any academic group incorporated under that name. The purest and deepest of human feelings make sharpest impression upon him and are the life-breath of several of his most moving poems. That with so many poets, from the author of Ecclesiastes to García Lorca, he is haunted by death, may be judged from "Sunday Morning." He is master of the elegy not as a preconceived poetic form but as poetic inspiration. Of this "Esthétique du Mal" gives the most impressive evidence. Two poignant little poems of bereavement also show both his tenderness and his delicate and most effective obliquity in his expression of man's feelings. These are

"Another Weeping Woman" and "The Weeping Burgher." The wound of the weeping woman is deepened by her failure to express her sorrow, by her inarticulateness, which, in turn, evinces her lack of a functioning imagination. To Stevens, the imagination signifies the core of vitality; it is human life both in the germ and in the flower. Excessive grief, grief uncontrolled, numbs whatever power of imagination its victim possesses. "Another Weeping Woman" announces the core of the first scene in Stevens' masterpiece, "Owl's Clover," where a woman in mourning is too strongly moved to be even so much as aware of the statue before which she stands. Especially in "Another Weeping Woman" brevity becomes pointedness and pointedness becomes poignancy. If the woman could only speak, she might be cured. The last line proves especially trenchant: "And you are pierced by a death." In such a piece wisdom joins hands with tenderness and pathos. Its force lies in a deceptive simplicity, a complete escape from spurious rhetoric, a most intense sincerity of tone.

"Another Weeping Woman" gives direct expression to the predicament of the bereaved. It voices the feminine penchant for emotional confession. That Stevens has this intention is even indicated in his title. Of such women there are, as he declares, "another, and another and another." "The Weeping Burgher," on the contrary, voices the imaginative paradoxes dear to the masculine mind in time of peculiar stress. The burgher, by whom we must to some extent understand Stevens himself, the smiling philosopher of "The Comedian as the Letter C," turns inward to laugh at himself. The laughter in this short poem proves considerably more bitter than that in the long work. The burgher has evidently been affecting to smile at his grief. Now he acts as the jesting clown with a broken heart, in the manner of the *commedia dell' arte*. This is a tragicomic poem of emotional complexes, the "weeping in a calcined heart." Stevens has great aptitude in the expression of such ironic experience. That the piece is in some respects autobiographical and the poet's own confession is further inferred from the phrase: "as ghost I come among the people burning in me still." In other words, he both addresses the people and speaks in behalf of his own fiery ordeals. Neither the poem's indirection nor its extreme artifice should conceal its sincere expression of violent feeling.

The depth of an emotion is often best measured by its refinement, or, in other words, by the sensibility which becomes a phase of it. Stevens' refined art in particular depends for its strength upon its delicacy or nuances. Since instances are far too many for enumeration, a particularly striking example must suffice. "A Woman Sings a Song for a Soldier Come Home," though not an easy poem to read appreciatively, affords a good instance of Stevens' technique, his capacity for feeling and his ability to express it. Nothing is overobvious. The title fits the poem like a glove but bears no literal relation to it. A man has suffered, whether in war or peace makes really little difference. He suffers still further in that he encounters heavy obstacles to the expression of his suffering. The experience causing his pain lies behind him in vague and monstrous forms, like piled-up thunderclouds. He cannot look forward and yet, in his unresolved state, dreads looking backward. Like another ancient mariner, he must remain enslaved to his tragic experience until the telling of it to a sympathetic person releases him. Society, the many, even an institution such as the Church, or professional aid such as the physician, cannot suffice. Only a friend and a state of privacy and intense intimacy can suffice, loosening his tongue and unburdening his heart. In fact, he hardly need speak; a gracious silence, with the understanding assumed, may be enough. Or to this may be added love itself, as Stevens intimates in the poem's closing words. The meeting may begin with words merely about the weather. It is well that it should occur "Just out of the village, at its edge, in the quiet there." The poem is in an intensely realized pianissimo, comparable in spirit to an andante in one of the later quartets by Beethoven. The very antithesis of melodrama, this is emotion *in excelsis*.

An emotion may be the intensification of a mood. Inextricably related even to the most violent passions is the sense of blankness, the emotion of no motion, the cessation of feeling in the numbness caused by extreme pain. This is the ultimate cold into which the sufferer is plunged by some desperate tragic frustration. To grasp this condition is to comprehend the emotional life as well as the meaning of the most violent experience. Poetry from Charles Baudelaire to T. S. Eliot has been much concerned with precisely this neurotic mood—one may even say, obsessed with it. Although Stevens is by no means overwhelmed by it, being essentially an idealist and not a defeatist, a robust and not a psychopathic figure, he knows its quality well, as anyone must who has at any time suffered the stronger impacts of feeling. It is as old as Sophocles' *Ajax*.

In Stevens' last volume there is a poem of only ten lines, "Vacancy in the Park," which shows an exquisite understanding of the mood in question. The allusion to a public place in the title delicately hints that the mood is prevalent in modern society. The loneliest people inhabit our most public places. Stevens contemplates desultory footprints wandering across the snow. They suggest to him a mood which is in turn conveyed to the reader by certain images. The prints are like a boat that has pulled away from a dock at night and vanished; like a guitar which a woman has forgetfully left on a table; most of all, they resemble the feelings of a man who returns to a vacant house with which in happier times he has had the most intimate associations. The man has lost something and does not even know precisely what he has lost. In short, the footprints in the snow prove to be not the main feature of the poem but only its inception. All the images are united to a single purpose, and presumably the last is the culminating image. This could be a poem of bereavement, through the loss of a dear relationship by either estrangement or death. It could be a symbolic expression of the loss of faith in life itself, or of God. Much remains deliberately and artfully unspecified. But the quality of the emotion is by no means unspecified. It is closely defined in a poem of much sensibility and force.

Similar insight is often shown in the expression of a happier mood and with the aid of a much more complex and extended imagery. "The Owl in the Sarcophagus" is such a piece, one of Stevens' outstanding works both in its emotional insights and its technical virtuosity. In a sense the poem is almost as dark as the interior of the sarcophagus itself; its imagery is of a dimness befitting the owl's vision. A master of color and vividness deliberately forgoes all color and brightness. Although the virtuosity is extreme, the sincerity remains incontestable, conveyed to no small degree by the somber, elegiac tone of the verse-music. Stevens attempts to capture the mood in which the modern man faces death, unaffected by either hopes of heaven or fears of hell. It is Stevens walking in Hamlet's graveyard. One must read the piece for its mood, conjured up by a unique and powerful imagination, not in search of any argument syllogistically presented. Although the work rests on a philosophic basis, its meaning transcends philosophy and ultimately rests in the heart. Stevens studies the emotions with the discernment of the very finest eye dissecting the heart's fibers. There is and there is not an allegory. No clear images are admitted into the twilight of the tomb, yet the presence of shadowy figures becomes all the more strongly felt. There are three major figures: sleep, peace, and death. With sleep and peace, Stevens includes rest and dreams: on the one hand, the stationary condition of ultimate repose, on the other, the restless conditions of the mind crowded with phantasms. Stevens recalls the infinite dreams with which man has invested a future life, the mythologies painted on the walls of tombs, the visions that live as art and emotional insights, though their power to convince theologically has long vanished. "What dreams may come / When we have shuffled off this mortal coil?" With insight comparable also to Prospero's apostrophe to dreams, Stevens likens all human thought to the fecundity of the dreaming mind. Death itself he conceives not, after Dürer's fancy, as the grim reality of the skeleton, nor as the journey to lands unknown which Hamlet envisaged with so much dread and trembling, but, much more simply, as saying farewell. Such poignance repeatedly shows itself as Stevens' finest emotional insight, his utmost tenderness, his most explicit and uncompromising humanity. Death here is mother not only of Beauty, as declared in "Sunday Morning," but of Memory.

> Keep you, keep you, I am gone, oh keep you as
> My memory, is the mother of us all.

This conjunction of the image of death and the mother proves one of the most daring imaginative feats of a poet distinguished for such boldness. Only through the very greatest emotional tenderness could it be achieved. His imagery in this poem, as in many of his strongest, also achieves its heights not in reference to customary symbols but, more humanly, to gestures. We have already seen this art in "Esthétique du Mal":

> Be near me, come closer, touch my hand, phrases
> Comprehended of dear relation, spoken twice,
> Once by the lips, once by the services
> Of central sense, these minutiae mean more
> Than clouds, benevolences, distant heads.

For a poet whose rhetoric had, as the speech of no other poet in English, captured the baroque majesty of clouds, this realization constituted a remarkable renunciation, confession, and spiritual revelation. In "The Owl in the Sarcophagus" we read of Death: "She spoke with the backward gestures of her hand." Such are gestures of a master in the consummate expression of emotion. His art came to its climax neither with bang nor whimper but with a firmly executed pianissimo. As the greatest of English poets declared, and as the composer of *The Passion According to Saint Matthew* knew equally well, "this is a manly sorrow."

XI : *The Hero*

WALLACE STEVENS by no means accords with the familiar description of the aesthete, the lover of beauty, who evades moral and ethical considerations. This is a point to be stressed, since his insistence on the prime value of artistic imagination and his assertions, generally in prose, that poetry is, ideally speaking, detached from politics, have led several of his critics to overlook one of the most important aspects of both his poetry and thought. He is made of much sterner stuff than may at first appear, and however much he relies on French avant-garde writers and delights in quoting wittily from the French, he remains at heart primarily a New Englander and an Anglo-Saxon. His aestheticism saves him from the moralistic tone of Matthew Arnold and even from the didactic tone encountered more or less frequently in Ezra Pound and T. S. Eliot, W. H. Auden and Stephen Spender; but the judge and critic of life is present in Stevens no less than the judge and critic of art. His ideas and idealism extend to both fields. He never, like William Blake, thinks of himself as a prophet in the ancient Hebraic tradition, but frequently refers to the philosophical poet as "rabbi," alluding to a more intellectual and sophisticated type of preceptor. His moralizing in poetry assumes a grand tone that accompanies a manner the majesty and aloofness of which may easily prove deceptive, for however far the head of this idealist reaches above the clouds, his feet remain on earth. This is itself a measure of his heroic or exalted stature, as yet, perhaps, inadequately estimated. Readers are today accustomed to recognize a critical voice by an irritability of tone or even by such hectic or perfervid excitement as is found in the writings of Ezra Pound and Hart Crane. Criticism is scarcely detected when expressed in elegant words and a relatively serene voice. Both the strategy of the demagogue and the nerves of the aesthete encourage a strident tone. We are much more accustomed to the morose or essentially pessimistic critic, whose execrations have extended from the frost-bitten vehemence of Herman Melville to the rain-soaked melancholy of Conrad Aiken. Stevens' critique is cast in a totally different mode, at times even vehement but always urbane.

A negative recognition of his seriousness, to be sure, has arisen from the genuine surprise of several of his own commentators who have obviously been impressed that a poet of the twentieth century and, even more specifically, of the generation of T. S. Eliot should frequently write of "the hero." The word certainly implies some moral judgment as well as moral idealism. Although a close investigation of Stevens' idea of the hero shows his thinking even here to be considerably more in accord with his aestheticism than might at first be assumed, the fact remains that he has subtilized quite legitimately the orthodox conception of the hero and in so doing departed to no negligible extent from the general trends of modern thought and poetry. Of course the idea, like the word itself, occurs in only a fraction of his poems; yet it is of substantial importance both for his poetry and for the contribution of his thought. Although the subject has been occasionally discussed, the refinements of his thinking make it still a profitable one and distinctly necessary in the approach to his mind and art. The idea of greatness, of an aristocracy of "major men," as he terms them, meant much to him. Only his fondness for abstraction ("it must be abstract") presumably deterred him from mentioning in his verse more names of great men as he conceived them. But he does, of course, mention Mozart, Picasso, and several artists, and writes as himself when in "Description without Place" he cogently alludes to Calvin, to Pablo Neruda, the poet, to Nietzsche, and to Lenin.

So many are the refinements and modulations of his thinking in almost all fields that a reader easily overlooks the simple germ from which any branch of his thought may spring. To begin with, the hero is not necessarily the poet, nor even the intellectual or moral poet, though this he is often found to be. Stevens used the word with special frequency at the time of the Second World War and in the years following in reference to the idea of the soldier. His inclination to large abstraction assisted him in developing this idea on broad lines, while his basic traditionalism and the conservative phase of his thinking led him to cherish the popular and, among poets and novelists, the somewhat old-fashioned term. Throughout his life his tendency was to feel as a radical and think as a conservative, to be with the avant-garde in sensibility and with the orthodox in philosophy. Most of his ideas derive directly from the nineteenth century and especially from the nineteenth-century idealists, while the nervous and the verbal aspects of his poetry spring from the most recent trends in feeling. More than appears from the surface of his highly metaphorical and at times almost cryptic style, he clings to ideas established at least a generation or two before him. Even Calvinism is close to him, as it is to most of the notable American poets of Southern extraction. He borrows a conception of the hero by no means far removed from that of Carlyle and Emerson, or even Lessing and Schiller, and modifies it to accord with nuances in the cultural climate of the mid-twentieth century.

By the hero he understands, so far as bare definition or the root-meaning is concerned, very much what any thoughtful person is likely to understand. A hero is a man who has lived in such a manner that mankind is conspicuously the better for his having been. This condition generally presumes an element of struggle. Any conspicuous action to this end is an act of heroism. The hero is the leader in the evolution of a humane civilization. By exhibiting a primitive type of heroism or struggle dedicated to a cause, any loyal soldier is in a measure the hero—all the more so, if the cause as well as the generous dedication is for the betterment of mankind. Hence history records a development in the idea of the hero: the soldier is the most primitive, though in reactionary thought he is still regarded as the only true type of hero; the thinker who advances sound values for his people, or the artist who bequeaths new insights into the soul's potentialities, is now discovered to be the most highly developed type of hero and should, accordingly, be the most honored. For honor is, of course, the hero's due though it may well be denied him both during and after his lifetime. In Stevens' severer eyes the romantic conception tended to the melodramatic. It is also clear that Stevens would not have followed Thomas Carlyle in his glorification of that archwarrior, Frederick the Great. Yet Stevens does not accept such values as the Chinese established, looking with bland disfavor upon the claim of the soldier. He uses the image of the soldier positively, not negatively, much as Charles Ives uses military songs as occasional material for his music inspired by New England thought. From a variety of sources he builds up his own idealistic conception, a piquant deviation from the pessimism of most of the chief poetry of his own times.

Stevens cherished his ideal, it would seem, partly because of his love for the classics themselves, in which the conception of the hero plays so large a part, and partly because of the direct heritage of romantic idealism. "Unless we believe in the hero," he writes, "what is there to believe in?" The ancient and more familiar notions he finds "archaic," good in themselves, memorable, and to be cherished, but on no account to be accepted as final. On them as a foundation we must erect our own new concepts of value. Hence most of his poems dealing with the hero abound in qualifications and modulations, working out his own complex view in the light of the less qualified views of the past. The notion of the hero he finds commonly derived from that of the embattled hero. Of leaders in science or statecraft he says little or nothing. In the hero in myth, as the religious leaders or the chief actors in classical mythology, he also shows peculiarly little interest. As bitter realist, he is more inclined to side with the soldier, especially because he sadly recognizes that he lives in a time when war in unprecedented scope confronts mankind. His fairly long poem "Examination of the Hero in a Time of War" proves in this respect typical. War confronts him with the harsh paradox that war itself is evil and the heroic soldier good.

Scarcely any poet has more successfully condemned the spurious or banal celebration of military heroism. The eleventh stanza of the poem just mentioned holds up war and its ideal of military regimentation to savage ridicule. The third stanza of Part Two in "Notes toward a Supreme Fiction," beginning "The great statue of General Du Puy," is an unsurpassed ridicule of false heroics, frozen in the image of banal public monuments. The breath-taking ridicule of the Italian armies in Ethiopia in "Owl's Clover" is unsurpassed of its kind. Typically, in "The Bouquet," already discussed, Stevens presents the figure of the soldier as the embodiment of coarse, unthinking, brutish insensibility.

One of his strongest poems, though one conceivably marred with overingenious phrasing, "Repetitions of a Young Captain," contrasts the ideal of the hopeful individualist with the tyranny of a communal ideal of military grandeur, now grown obsolete and false. The false idea is the idealization of war in the sense that war is in itself a satisfying or "real" world. The emotionally unsatisfying or essentially frustrating in life is here not improperly described as "unreal." To a man whose emotional life and spiritual ideals are uprooted, life inevitably becomes unreal. A thoroughly hostile environment tends to become such. War itself today resembles a bad dream, a play of horrors that may vanish as dramatically as a stage-picture

must vanish if the roof of a theater blows off. Modern war
is commonly beyond the assimilation of the imagination.
The common soldier, at least, lives within it as in a dream.
Or perhaps much in our modern life seems to the unimaginative essentially unreal, as to the imaginative it appears essentially grotesque and perverse. These are the
unrealities, spiritually considered. The "real" person is
one who has assimilated his life imaginatively and balanced the tensions of his emotions; he is the true hero, the
leader of mankind out of an uncivilized darkness. To know
that modern war is essentially incredible is the beginning
of modern civilized wisdom. War has always been hell but
today it is also chaos.

In "Examination of the Hero in a Time of War" occurs
a further idea or development of the foregoing. This is the
hero's anonymity. The hero is today thought of as a spokesman or even merely a symbol for his society rather than
as its leader. We live in the leaderless age of the unknown
soldier. This thought springs from the conception of the
hero "in time of war," when as far as the military ideal is
concerned, the communal need is more conspicuous than
the imagination of the individual. In designating his
farthest limit of fruitful individualism, Stevens commonly
omits the word "leader" or any such term whatsoever, pre-
ferring his own coinage, "major man," synonymous with
"the hero." This conception of the major man is his understanding of the imaginative man laboring the most successfully in the interests of our common humanity. The
contrast between the major man and the military ideal at
its best is vividly expressed in "Gigantomachia." This is a
poem based on qualifications. In it war is described as en-
larging the mind to the extent to which it effects petty

aspects of the personal life. Certain large, simple conceptions take the place of these trifling views. But this new
world conceived in spacious proportions is in itself crude,
gigantic, uncivilized, unrefined. The typical soldier carries
no appreciable load of thought or understanding. Although some of life's tragic aspects in the archaic sense
are forced upon him, as the imminence of death, the infinite scope of the true and truly powerful imagination
lies unspeakably removed from him. In the ironical words
of the poem's final line, "For soldiers, the new moon
stretches twenty feet."

A kinder view of the soldier as hero appears in "Dutch
Graves in Bucks County," where a likeness is found between early American settlers, chiefly concerned with
religious freedom, and modern soldiers enlisted in a democratic cause primarily dedicated to the more political freedoms. The poem is in many ways an exception to Stevens'
more usual reflections. As he confesses in an after-com-
ment in prose in his war-time volume, *Parts of a World*,
times of war are unfavorable to his ideals for modern
poetry. They place the poet in an awkward position, push-
ing him toward the more conservative and communal
realizations of life. "The major man" flourishes best in
times congenial to the utmost freedom of expression.
Under these circumstances his more refined and forward-
looking perceptions may the more readily be cultivated
and understood by his public. Thunder of modern warfare, Stevens finds, has a strident voice drowning out the
bolder absolutes and generalizations essential in his conception of ideal art, which, in his own words, must itself
"be abstract."

Hence if we seek the meaning of his own view of the

"hero," or "major man," we do best to turn away from his poems heavily darkened by the shadow of war. He gives us, in fact, only a few elegies for wartime victims, fine as these elegies are. Perhaps "Esthétique du Mal" may be regarded as such a poem. Its strophe commencing "How red the rose that is the soldier's wound" may be considered one of the most moving memorial verses written in our times. Likewise the brief poem "Flyer's Fall" has great chastity, nobility, and distinction. This is the almost perfect modern elegy, free from the orthodox view of immortality or any orthodox political views. Its six lines have a richness of thought and phrase, a quiet dignity and spiritual conviction, a music for the spirit, which quite escapes adequate description. That the flyer was a hero in life we are not assured but we are completely convinced that he was a hero in death, that he knew his death to be heroic, and that in contemplating his clean, instant, and wordless death the poet, or master of a few chosen words, has himself conquered an area for heroic awareness. Life becomes heroic in the realization of such a moment both in the flyer's career and the poet's austere thought. The truly heroic in life is life's true dignity, the antithesis of the parody of that dignity as seen in the pretentious rhetorical statue of General du Puy, in "Notes toward a Supreme Fiction."

The hero, according to Stevens, is the master of life, the "yea sayer," and yet more than that. It is not enough, in his view, to say yes to some divine or overmastering authority, as Christians are taught in resignation to say, "Thy will be done," or as an unthinking leader merely confirms with emphasis some established belief. Stevens goes beyond Carlyle in optimism. In Stevens' eyes the positive is more than merely the affirmative. Its impulse must come from within, a creation as well as an affirmation, an awareness of well-being amounting almost to gusto. Thus the hero, or major man, is well defined by a brief poem, "The Brave Man." The description is purely symbolic. "That brave man" is none other than the sun rising in splendor and serene assurance. He comes through boughs that lie in wait, disperses invidious, gloomy apparitions; even anemic goodness and personal turpitude flee his face. He asserts himself in action and intuition, leaving meditation to others. This little poem is as subtle as the thought of Rilke, as elemental as that of Blake. It admirably describes Stevens' conception of the heroic.

The hero, then, is one who has confidently found the road to the richest living. Invariably Stevens prefers to express this idea in so abstract a manner that it shall be elusive to the critical intellect but gratifying to the spiritual imagination. Good evidence of this is the poem "How to Live, What to Do." In its twenty lines the word "heroic" appears only twice, once in the first and in the last quatrain, yet the word clearly states the mood and meaning of the entire piece. On one level this is a love poem. Two persons are depicted on a naked height of rock, described as tufted in the sense that it has trees at its base: "bosomed high on tufted trees," to use Milton's phrase, which may have been in the back of Stevens' mind as he wrote. The two lovers look out with clear, cold eyes upon the highly imperfect world lying at their feet. They stand well above and removed from the habitations of common men. In the night only the giant forms are visible: the hills, the clouds, the rocks. The two are motionless, unattended by ornament, by chorister, or by priest.

The sun with its freckled splendors is left far beyond them. Best of all, there is the loud voice of a cold wind, "joyous and jubilant and sure." These two at least for a time have risen to heroic stature. They are heroes in a profounder sense than even the flyer fallen, one presumes, in war.

Stevens' heroic positivism is further characteristically expressed in a somewhat elusive, symbolical poem entitled, "On the Adequacy of Landscape." (The title, which might as cogently have been affixed to half the poems that Stevens wrote, signifies that to the man of imagination the landscape is quite adequate to symbolize whatever insight he requires.) For its central image the poet chose a small red owl hurtling through the night, to the consternation of birds and other creatures, frightened by the sudden whirring of its wings. Although Stevens can hardly be said to have made this image of the owl one of the major symbols in his poetry, he occasionally returns to it, so that this poem, in which it is first and most fully developed, acquires a special interest.

The bright young bird flying through the night, to the consternation of other creatures, both larger and smaller, symbolizes the appearance of the man of imagination in a darkened world, where his words and deeds disturb ordinary men, who almost instinctively, or possibly by dint of training, fear the distinctive or unusual. The owl is hero not only of the poem but of Stevens' world. Against him are pitted the victims of the unreal. The owl is lusty. Those who appreciate this bird of night are, in counterpoint to the main line of imagery, red-blooded persons, lovers of the "redness of the sun." Here, as elsewhere, Stevens associates red with courage and emotional strength. Those who dislike or fear the owl are the weak, revolted by his lusty cry and vigorous, startling action. Indeed, they fear any painful experience whatsoever. The owl, like the faithful thinker and true poet, on the contrary, is without fear of pain. The tragic becomes his element. This renders him so much the more a symbol of the hero, who struggles and endures, who, encountering both opposition and pain, has mastered them. This bird of ruddy courage Stevens kept in his heart. It instructed him in new definitions of heroism, befitting a world outgrowing its old conceptions and desperately in need of ideals to be defended not principally on battlefields but in fields of daily life.

XII : *Public Conditions, Social, Political, and Historical*

Aᴌᴛʜᴏᴜɢʜ some of Stevens' own statements on the relation between poetry and the public or political life appear contradictory, now establishing a rigid divorce and now admitting close relationship, his practice in his poetry cannot be held ambiguous. Generalizations on public problems he accepts freely as material for art; propaganda and detail he rigidly rejects. Despite his compulsion to explore poetics and metaphysics, he often becomes the forceful critic of organized society. He admitted that he had written some satirical and occasional poems. It must be obvious to any reader that his mind by no means stops short with his favorite metaphysical and psychological problems. In fact, he launches upon a powerfully imaginative social criticism, with an eye for conduct possessed only by a master of comedy and a particularly capable understanding of historical evolution. His poetry in this vein is as a rule nonpartisan, supporting no faction, program, or scheme of action. Being anything but an anarchist, he assumes the need of such programs, which serve urgent and specific purposes. But the artist he conceives as dealing with the particular only to mold abstractions. Hence the poet and politician have common interests but rarely meet in his verses. They view the same mountain from different angles. His views of our social predicaments and conditions are broad, imaginative, and penetrating. Much of his most vigorous poetry falls within this category.

This part of his work might have received more attention had it not been for his own qualifying attitude: he was inclined to look askance upon this aspect of his own achievement. His foremost objection was by no means that poetry should shun morality, but that at its best it must shun the topical. An idealist in most senses of the word, he disliked whatever he feared might confine or restrict the relevance of art. Recondite allusions he did not fear but topicality he shunned almost instinctively. That social themes at times left him uncomfortable as a poet appears in his attitude toward his own long and studiously composed "Owl's Clover." On its second publication he revised and abridged it, particularly weeding out a few topical remarks. When, close to the time of his own death, *The Collected Poems of Wallace Stevens* appeared, this was by far the most conspicuous omission. Possibly he felt the work marred not only by direct allusions to economic, political, and even artistic events, but by the rhetorical manner that he shunned in his later years. In any case, the poem was omitted. This must seem to many readers regrettable, since it is almost certainly one of the strongest among his long poems, a group which includes "Esthétique du Mal," "The Comedian as the Letter C," "Notes toward a Supreme Fiction," and "An Ordinary Evening in New Haven." This study commenced with an analysis of "Esthétique du Mal." It will conclude with an analysis of "Owl's Clover," one of the most difficult and most brilliant of his works. Many short poems, also, have a large public vision. The fine texture of his thought is found in these pieces as well as in the longest of his socially oriented works.

Although Stevens' retreat from downright propaganda in the Shavian manner accompanies a tendency to fatalism in his view of public affairs, he is by no means without judgment of them. This is seen in a poem so witty as almost to outsmart itself. "Forces, the Will & the Weather" shows his surprisingly skeptical view of capitalistic or American society. The noble thinker, "the peer yellow," sighs that neither he nor his countrymen have vigorous ideas:

> There was not an idea
> This side of Moscow. There were anti-ideas
> And counter-ideas. There was nothing one had.

In place of a society exercising political intelligence, the world which the poet actually observes is largely sentimental. To his meditative eye it resembles a lush spring landscape with sheets of the blossoms of pink and white dogwood, like sugar candy. Among these trees walks a young girl dragged along by a white poodle. By similar necessity, people are dragged along a path unthinking and without a plan, in a world at best pretty but unintelligent and destined to pass. The decorative world of the stupid girl will go down to defeat before the more substantial if less engaging world of the innovators. A new era is about to be inaugurated, as a waiter brings in fresh foods on a tray. The future is only to be awaited. This is a crisp, distinctly clever and memorable poem, no masterpiece, perhaps, but clear indication of a mind with considerable aptitude for social thinking and an eye for social revolutions.

Like so many poets and other men as well in our nervously apprehensive times, Stevens broods over the advent of some great catastrophe, probably a war, possibly only a social or economic calamity. "Girl in a Nightgown" proves one of the most poignant and imaginative realizations of this condition. No figure could better represent the helplessness with which millions of thoughtful persons await the menace of approaching storm. A young girl, clad only in her nightgown, faces a society armed to the teeth and threatening destruction of its own members and its own culture. Whether the chief threat comes from nationalistic wars or a social revolution, the poet does not state. His purpose is to represent a mood or state of consciousness arising from a condition only too widely recognized. For days rumblings have been heard from the horizon. Times are changing, and for the worse. There should be a condition of peace, with flute music heard under the summer boughs. But a spring rich in promise has yielded a winter full of fears. "It will burst into flames, either now or tomorrow or the day after that." The poem is firm in diction and eminently moving. Some of the thought and imagery resembles verse written at approximately the same time by British poets, as Auden, Spender, MacNeice and Day Lewis, but it would be hard to find so moving a statement in their laxer idiom. Stevens' poetry is less explicit but more suggestive, less journalistic but more creative. This distinction of Stevens' style promises well for its enduring.

Many poets have recently lifted their voices in grim

social prophecy, among them Robinson Jeffers, in whose verses a raven is forever boding destruction. To this concerted cry of warning Stevens adds his own clearer tones. "One of the Inhabitants of the West" is such a work. The poet sees an evening star as menacing as the star of the Wise Men was auspicious. The star speaks its message in oracular vein:

> Horrid figures of Medusa,
> These accents explicate
> The sparkling fall of night
> On Europe, to the last Alp,
> And the sheeted Atlantic.

The martial star flashes like a drop of blood against the background of a serene evening sky. Israel does not fall without guilt. Europe in its autumnal ripeness may seem innocent, but it is not innocent of the causes threatening its downfall. Still gazing at the star, the spirit of prophecy concludes:

> Suppose it was a drop of blood . . .
> So much guilt lies buried
> Beneath the innocence
> Of autumn days.

The indictment has a Biblical force. Like other oracles, it remains cryptic; all its lines are not equally effective; but it undeniably shows an inspired imagination at work upon a public theme.

A finer poem, "Martial Cadenza," interprets a brighter star in war time with a happier connotation for its viewer. This is a poem of mood, also of conversion, as well as a testimonial of the human condition in time of war or revolution. Stevens feels war as a period of defeat for man-

kind, a world experiencing disaster, fallen as a dead body
falls or as a winter night without hope of relief. Living in
this world of spiritual paralysis, he sees one evening low
in the sky the star that will crown every western horizon
in spring. Abruptly the clock of life that had stopped to
record both the personal and the public life begins to
move. Life takes on joyousness, hopefulness, infinite po-
tency. A world without spiritual meaning suddenly becomes a world of the most intense meaning. The speaker
has also experienced a resurrection. Stevens' words have
the sensitivity of music in rising to this essentially lyric or
dramatic thought. The first stanza is weighted with grief,
dark with despairing melancholy; the last flashes with the
most brilliant joy. Here is a poem of the highest merit,
obviously occasioned by the poet's reactions to the social
and political scene.

To this area of imagination or poetic understanding
should be added as well the economic world. "Idiom of
the Hero," without discouraging the reformer, warns him
that no millennium of bliss is possible in a persistently
imperfect world. Two houses, the poem declares, will always be more or less in conflict: the great and the mean,
the powerful and the weak, the rich and the poor. Although their relations may change, the dichotomy cannot
be ended. The poet concludes that life presupposes an un-
ending struggle within society, the ultimate satisfaction
resting in the individual and his capacity to surmount inevitable social injustice. The red and the white houses will
always be in conflict. The War of the Roses was compounded but this deeper conflict will not be compounded.
Above this strife, as above the benighted struggles of na-
tionalist powers, shines the star of poetic imagination and

the more enduring values which it signifies. In these lines Stevens assumes for himself the position of the Bohemian poet whose fortunes lie with the poor. His own case, politically considered, "cannot be amended." The poem consists of seven couplets, each of which concludes with the rhyme first announced as "ended." The syllable tolls like a bell. It is a master stroke in poetic form.

Sometimes Stevens sees the military and economic problems in conjunction, as in the powerful "Dry Loaf." Fatality dominates this work as well as the preceding, for it is inferred that war comes inevitably and inevitably impoverishes the common people. In its execution the work employs a well-known form of counterpoint. Flocks of drab birds, coming in waves, pass like evil auguries over somber mountains. So the soldiers march in waves over the land to the monotonous roll of their sinister drums. This is a wry, bitter poem with strong lyrical movement and vigorous expression of feelings only too familiar throughout the modern world.

By no means all Stevens' poems on social themes are focused on the two outstanding features of American public life at the time of his most important writings: first, the world wars and threats of wars; second, the economic depression and unrest. Several pieces are even less topical and more general. "A Thought Revolved" is such, almost certainly less striking as a poem than many others but decidedly of interest because of its thought and the sharp pointedness of a number of its lines. The piece is typical of Stevens in being essentially four variations on a single theme or four comparable poems in one. The first and possibly the best describes a sentimental woman of middle age with no mental capacity and boundless optimism. It announces the theme: the search for leadership in the modern world. This fashionable lady elects Santa Claus, the leader who gives without stint or reservation, the fairy godfather. By way of contrast, the second section proposes the dry, rationalistic leader who follows tradition, dispenses with the externals of Virgilian decorum but wishes to conserve the essence of classicism. This looks much like a gentle satire on the "New Humanists." No indication is given that Stevens himself discerns a political panacea along these essentially reactionary lines. The second "variation" is no resounding finale. The dignity and decorum of the state are asserted but little enthusiasm or spiritual conviction is expressed. The third variation presents, again in sharp contrast, the ultraromantic ideal of the leader, the hero, revered even in his lifetime as a saint but fundamentally not of this world, so that the people whom he leads become victims of his own irrational views. Rulers such as this, the poet suggests, have come from Poland, a country singularly victimized by such misguided governors. The statesman should not be the singer or the artist. Public affairs demand a methodology of their own. This section provides a satirical elegy for such a leader as Paderewski.

The final section depicts a leader along lines of the baroque age or such lines as modern partisans of that period espouse. The imagery is in part quixotic: the passage describes a "moralist hidalgo." He proves himself another in the line of impractical idealists, a victim of doctrinaire or bookish notions. (There is a possible glance at the reactionary politics of Ezra Pound.) This imaginary statesman dreams heroic dreams in the Spanish fashion, while, like Spanish leaders of all descriptions, he is actually surrounded by squalor. There is some fundamental defect in his power to grasp reality. He resembles a man with some abnormal physical distortion, a preposterous foot or toe. So four types of persons dream of four types of public leadership, all following will-o'-the-wisps of illusion. Throughout, this fourfold poem shares equally in the moods of satire and the grotesque.

Stevens' preference for abstraction continually pulls him away from politics toward philosophy, leaving him often in a fruitful region midway between the two. He enjoys large ideas comprehending both public and private affairs, the principles of government and those of art. One of his more remarkable poems, first published in 1945, illustrates this tendency. "Recitation after Dinner," as its title suggests, is couched with considerable skill in tones of polite talk. But this proves to be part of the poet's conspiracy, the shrewdness of his long-experienced strategy. After some conversational comments of an intellectual character and negative conclusions explaining what tradition is not, at a carefully calculated moment the poem reaches its real excuse for being. The epic symbol for which Stevens designed this colloquial frame is one of the most memorable in all his works and actually one of the most often remembered. Tradition, he declares, is signified by the hero Aeneas carrying out of burning Troy his father Anchises on his shoulders. This is true tradition, not merely memory, nor an intellectual order, nor an historical inevitability, nor a forced preservation of forms, but a vital, passionate relation between past and present, where the present establishes its superior power yet venerates and loves its live heritage. Tradition may even be established upon historical error. It is an impersonal reality sustained with personal sentiment. "Recitation after Dinner" is a unique production. Only a poet of Stevens' stature could harmonize, as his reflective style certainly does harmonize, colloquial discourse and epic image, uniting the humanity of the one with the nobility of the other, preserving the one from meanness and the other from ostentation. The more the poem is studied, the more distinguished it is found to be.

Sometimes Stevens' focus of attention on the public life passes downward to his local Connecticut, which he commonly views with affection. A lesser poem of this sort, "Of Hartford in a Purple Light," has many qualities of light verse yet is no more witty than discerning. He reflects on the revolution that has come over the society of his home city, once so strongly masculine a community, now in so much of its cultural atmosphere feminine, cosmopolitan, and French. The sun, he reflects, has been traveling a long time from Havre to Hartford but of late more than sunlight has followed this course. An older America, even in far-off Pasadena, has turned from Anglo-Saxon byways to cosmopolitan highways. The French poodle has invaded our land. Stevens views the change with pleasurable detachment. On the whole, it seems to him a gain, for he, too, loves the French, dog and man. This discerning poem is an engaging product of his comic muse.

A finer piece, "Reality Is an Activity of the Most August Imagination," celebrates what he regards as the firmness and substantiality of the New England imagination, to which he rightly regards himself as attached. The lines are highly imagistic. As he drives home from Cornwall to Hartford, he sees a celestial display; the night sky is lit with gorgeous colors that appear solids, although they change rapidly and in time dissolve. In comparison with the glow of glassworks in Venice or Vienna these lights are both more mobile and more dense. Time gathers no dust on them. The glories of New England skies provide ever-refreshing springs of inspiration symbolizing the insights of the New England mind. His images are eclectic, mysterious, almost unique. They brilliantly symbolize several qualities in New England pragmatism and idealism, both of which Stevens finds much to his liking.

Although such minor poems as these cover a wide range in his speculations on public problems and affairs, his chief excursion into these fields, as already noted, is the long and exceptionally difficult work "Owl's Clover," with ingenious symbolism, profuse imagery, heavily loaded aphorism, and much rhetorical eloquence devoted to many aspects of aesthetic, social, political, and historical thought. A companion to the task of reading and digesting such a poem can hardly be unwelcome. "Owl's Clover" is one of the most rewarding flights of Stevens' art. Although its diverse parts may not be completely harmonized, the work gathers a force scarcely equaled by any of his other poems. The view of life which it presents is unmistakably social. Where the individual is examined, he is invariably viewed in relation to his culture, socially and historically considered. The psychological insights merge into the public scene. Stevens examines his views of art in relation to history and to society.

From almost all possible viewpoints, "Owl's Clover" is a difficult work, demanding analytical study and repaying it. Even in the light of such poems as have just been examined, the reader is unprepared for so long and imposing a work. Its transitions are rough; its basic symbols highly unusual; its metaphorical expressions so profuse as to be almost bewildering. Reading it resembles a walk through a dense wood: there is always much close to the eye to attract attention, with little opportunity to secure an over-all view, and an enormous amount of detail to remember. The astonishing passage on the African jungle in Part Three seems in an odd way symbolical of the whole. There is no poem which the present writer has read so often and few which he has found so gratifying.

Its witty title notwithstanding, "Owl's Clover" is a very serious composition. It may best be described as an essay on civilization, past, present, and future. The prospect extends widely on every side, with vistas into psychology, human geography, politics, history, economics, theology, and almost all the major divisions of speculative thought. At the center, as almost always with Stevens, stands his theory of art. But this theory is itself so philosophical and the relations of art to other aspects of thought and activity are found so vital and so intricate, that the poem's central problem is too readily misjudged. Actually, Stevens' view of art is of central importance to his view of life and key to his metaphysics. Art he finds man's most important gateway to reality and the central activity in establishing a civilization. As here conceived, it is a means not to pleasure or relaxation but to the most adequate awareness of life. It is regarded as basic; politics, morality, with our other chief fields of thought and activity, are built upon it, or, from another angle, its manifestations are at any given time conditioned by the attendant cultural factors, coming in art to their highest fruition. Art is both fruit and flower.

The central image of the poem, upon which this examination of art is focused, is a sculptural group of horses located in a park in some unspecified northern city. This group is present in all five of the poem's short Books, or Parts, but appears and disappears in a somewhat confusing manner. It resembles a public monument of the school of Bernini, in short, of the baroque period. The choice of this symbol may be explained as follows. Poetry, as Stevens conceives it, proceeds from concrete image to abstract idea. An image is demanded. The baroque period stands centrally located in the historical world which the poem explores. Neither at the beginning nor at the end of Western civilization, which is Stevens' chief theme, but *in medias res*, it offers a strategic starting point from which to deploy. Moreover, the baroque is itself one of the major periods of art, pre-eminent in music and of much importance in painting, sculpture, drama, and architecture. Stevens felt compelled to begin with a specific reference and this proved especially agreeable to him. At this point it should be added that Part One has its scene in the present—the statue is primarily seen in our own times. Book Five, or the last Book, is chiefly concerned with the future. The first half of Book Two glances at the Romantic period. Book Four is occupied largely with the present. Book Three, entitled "The Darkest Continent," makes an imposing digression into primitive Africa, in the manner of so much art and speculation on aesthetics during the early years of the present century, with the vogue of African art in Paris and Berlin and the use of it made by Picasso and his associates, both in painting and sculpture. In Book Three Stevens also observes, neither with peculiar grief nor satisfaction, the fall of Europe. Other cultures

than the modern European and other parts of the globe
loom in new and imposing importance. Hence Africa, in
Book Three, serves as well as any other continent to give
the poem the desired breadth of horizon.

Taken as a whole, "Owl's Clover" must be regarded as
a long verse-essay comprising a sequence of five essays on
the nature and history of civilization. Like its title, it is
rich in fantasy and the grotesque, which in no way reduce
the essential seriousness which is certainly intended. In it
is a little of Aristophanes, a little of Quevedo, and something of Goya. At least the "portent," the mysterious
figure in Book Five, has a striking likeness to that magic
print of the Colossus, one of Goya's last and most mysterious works. There is no smooth sequence of ideas or
of images. Inasmuch as all civilization is spread before
the poet's eyes, the reader must be prepared at almost any
moment for a reference or allusion to any time, place, or
event in history. To plunge into such a poem presents a
certain risk and not too sanguine a promise for the reader's
satisfaction. On this account, before a book-by-book or
page-by-page analysis is offered, some further remarks on
its general character, spirit, and intention should be useful.

Probably the nearest approximation to it in English
literature—though the comparison cannot, of course, be
pushed to extremes—is offered by Alexander Pope's *Dunciad*. Contrasts and comparisons here may prove enlight-
ening. To place the two works side by side in the mind is
to realize graphically something of the contrast between
past and present which Stevens himself delineates. The
Augustan world looks surprisingly simple and self-con-
tained; the modern world, precariously complex and un-

resolved. Pope's horizons appear rigorously limited. The well-defined forms and ideas of classical satire constitute the organizing features of his work. Allusions seem almost parochial. Pope contrives to make poetry of lasting interest out of his peevish quarrels and personal relations within the comparatively small literary circle of the London of his day. As his subjects are clear, so is his verbal expression lucid. The poem is a transparency. Like Mozart's music, it has infinite nuances imposed upon an essential clarity of line. Though it can be reread almost indefinitely, it is thoroughly straightforward. In most of these respects it stands at the opposite pole from "Owl's Clover." The similarities between the two cast equal light upon the work struggling in darkness. Both poems are verse-essays on the spirit of the times, focused primarily upon aesthetic issues. Both are episodic and discursive, with a brilliant rhetorical development of the verse paragraph. Both proceed through modes of satire and the grotesque to an odd variant of the tragic mode; both conclude with a somewhat forced but aesthetically powerful prophecy of comprehensive degeneracy of taste and decay of imagination. So much alike in essence are the last page of *The Dunciad* and the last page of "Owl's Clover" that I find it difficult to believe that the American poet had not at least in the back of his mind a recollection of his predecessor in this general field of discursive and reflective verse.

No owl or clover is, of course, mentioned in Stevens' poem. His treatment of the central image, the statue, gives a fair indication of his philosophical point of view. The entire poem is in a sense an exercise, an experiment. Stevens devised the statue as his leading symbol and undertook the task of turning it about for the most comprehensive scrutiny, observing it through the eyes of different types of persons and different centuries, lands, and even continents. With the legerdemain of a master geometrician, he assumes it standing in the African jungles, in a remote past, in a remote future; he imagines it as seen from beneath by dwarfish men, or as seen from a far height in the air. In an age of relativity, the relativity of the impressions and conclusions of the mind can in this manner be suggested and explored. But one difficulty of his poem is that the statue provides only a single theme with its variations; Stevens' plan demanded many subsidiary themes as well and tangential passages that nevertheless explicate the dominant idea, which is the course of the aesthetic imagination through the ages, the chief emphasis falling upon the poet's own age and the future which ominously overshadows it. The reader must perceive that "Owl's Clover" has no simple development, as did "The Comedian as the Letter C," which is merely the biography of a poet's style. He may be thankful that the statue provides a thread through the labyrinth, but must also be aware that the piece explores far more than is specifically laid on the broad shoulders of the marble horses.

That Stevens' theme is predominantly social is clarified by the location of the statue in a public park, a park, no doubt, in the grand baroque design of landscape gardening, as the statue itself appears baroque. This image of the park comes much closer to a poetic orthodoxy than that of the statue. Many poets have employed it or its equivalent, especially if one enlarges the conception to include spacious outdoor public meeting places with some element of landscape design, as town commons and great public squares, where fairs, festivals, and large assemblies are held. The outdoor scenes in the first act of Goethe's *Faust* and in the last act of *Die Meistersinger* would be instances. One could well go back as far in time as the "Fair Field Full of Folk" in Langland's *Piers Plowman*, or consider a work as recent as Sean O'Casey's brilliant *Within the Gates*, where that romantic playwright assumes a classical form. Stevens' poem, then, deals with the masses of men, yet his philosophy instructs him that the individual is the quintessence of the mass and that a single gesture or an uplifted arm may mean more than a panorama with thousands of figures.

Part One begins with the description of the statue, the particular work of art shrewdly selected to stand for all art and to carry so much of the weight of the argument. Before it he places not a crowd but a solitary figure, a woman, so absorbed in her private emotions, in this instance deep melancholy, that the statue and its joyous energy signify nothing whatsoever to her. It is night, the time of imagination, but it is also a time of darkness in the woman's soul. Stevens develops here an idea powerfully expressed also in "Esthétique du Mal," and others of his poems, namely, that a work of art can be appreciated only by the viewer who resigns his more personal feelings and becomes absorbed in the microcosm presented to him. This by no means signifies that the individual must not bring appropriate intelligence and sensitivity to bear upon the work, or that his final appreciation will not remain in a sense personal, but simply that romantic egocentricity cannot intrude upon a fully developed aesthetic experience.

The scene in Book One extends its meaning, however, somewhat further. Rather by implication than by statement, it is inferred that the woman's misery is caused by a malaise in society itself, of which she is the victim. No narrow social or economic explanation proves adequate to the passage, and some commentaries describing the scene wholly in these terms, as of the great American economic depression, may actually indicate a defective appreciation of Stevens' intention. Still, many women, grieving at their own unemployment and that of their husbands thronged American parks at the time of Stevens' writing. This he certainly knew. But in any event, the scene declares in essence that society must provide a condition of comfort and assurance before art, which is both a luxury and a necessity, can fulfill its true function. All of Part One is written with great energy; the lines on the statue excel in virtually epic force; those on the grieving woman are a Euripidean conjunction of tragic feeling and lyrical pathos. As Stevens depicts the woman, she fails to understand her own grief and therefore fails to master it. She lacks the power to comprehend either herself or the statue beside her. Her defect is a want of poetic imagination.

With Part Two, or "Mr. Burnshaw and the Statue," panaceas alleged to cure the plight of such sufferers as the unhappy woman are considered. The title refers to an article by Stanley Burnshaw, with a Marxist inspiration, which appeared in the leftist periodical *The New Masses*, October 1, 1935. As Stevens interpreted this article, Burnshaw favored art's servitude to the state, an outlook especially repugnant to the New England poet, who in the fourth section of "Owl's Clover" makes still another attack on Soviet art and aesthetics with a slur at the current vogue for propagandistic music, expressive of the stridencies of a mechanistic culture. The type of abstract political idealism behind such work especially offended Stevens, who disliked all millennial dreaming. This thought leads him to speculations on Shelley and others of this description.

Having castigated the vague idealisms of these assorted visionaries as inimical to the sound art symbolized by the statue, the poem turns abruptly to an antithetical attitude, that of the rigid conservative who resents all change. This attack on absolutism and rigidity is typical of Stevens' thought in all periods of his writing and in poems short or long, as "A High-Toned Old Christian Woman" and "It Must Change," the second section in "Notes toward a Supreme Fiction." In short, the true value of the statue escapes equally the visionary, whose thoughts gather wholly about the future, and the unimaginative conservative, who in his love for the past resents innovation of any sort. Since all true art is to some extent innovation, the second attitude is false from its very beginning. Substantiating a truism, Stevens elaborates the notion that all things decay, thus refuting the position of the unbending conservative, whose attitude typifies the static mind of senility. Its antithesis is presented as a primitive emotionalism. In the original version of "Owl's Clover," Part Two ends with a description of an ecstatic primitive ritual, similar to the account in the next to the last stanza of "Sunday Morning." This orgiastic ritual is interpreted as closer to the spirit of true art, or the statue, than the poetic dreams of any group enamored of the future or the bloodless repetitions of essentially uncreative reactionaries. Art, Stevens insists, must be faithful to the realities of life, a goal which he finds unrealized by Communist art, millennial art, or academic art. Throughout Part

Two the level of style remains high, but the logical thread of the argument notwithstanding, the passages seem episodic, the reasoning is seduced by antitheses, and the statue is allowed to pass too far into the background.

Part Three, "The Greenest Continent," is stylistically the most brilliant section of "Owl's Clover." Art, religion, and relativity are among its chief themes. A powerful verse-paragraph at its beginning rationalizes the shift of scene to Africa with a picture of culture in contemporary Europe as fundamentally decadent. Europe is described as failing to survive its loss of religious faith. Africa, on the contrary, is described as having gods only too real but unfriendly to both life and art, since they exist as images of terror and fear. Stevens clearly feels the religions of highly civilized peoples to be friendly to art but is skeptical of theology. A discussion appropriately imagined to take place in a café argues that modern art should be wholly human and that at least in our own age it deserts its true object in celebrating gods. Besides, our religion, along with our ideals, has become vastly distorted. In a passage of dazzling caricature, Stevens depicts the Italian aviators in the Ethiopian war as angels of the modern world engaged in grotesque and futile conflict with the primitives. This religion of debased materialism and nationalism merits only scorn. He discovers but one god truly convincing to the modern mind—Ananke, or fate. Fate alone placed the statue in its place of origin and decrees that it cannot be transported into the world of primitivism. Elsewhere, he expresses faith in a religion close to art, where each man realizes for himself, without aid of an established theology, the values that to him are most convincing. As many poems in *Harmonium* and "The Idea of

Order at Key West" show, Stevens' imagination was powerfully enkindled by the tropics. This subject matter is
given its final and strongest glow in this section of "Owl's
Clover."

Part Four distinguishes the lasting values of any sound
work of art from those no less essential values that relate
it to the legitimate needs of time and place. In short, this
is the creed of an idealist who is also a believer in relativity. It asserts the need for a modern art adapted to
modern conditions and characterized by a hopeful outlook both for art itself and for society, whose well-being
and culture must always be attuned to developments in
the arts. In this section thought roams over a wide arc
from past to future, maintaining its fulcrum in the present.
Beneath the present lies the promise of the rise of labor,
or the common man, and that of his alleged spokesmen,
the Communist leaders. This condition is broached in
the first twenty lines. But throughout the world, in both
Communist and capitalist lands, appear many signs menacing the course of civilization. In any case, the buskin
age of the pioneer has passed. The past is gone but the
present is almost as baffling as the future. Precisely where
we stand is described as problematical. On the one hand,
the imagination is threatened by the vexing isolation of
the individual, both as man and as artist; on the other
hand, by his subjugation to the stupidities of the mass
mind. A powerful passage describes in these terms the
degeneration in the life of modern cities. Rays of hope,
however, are found in the imaginative efforts occasionally
discovered in "major men" to explore the possibilites of
the future. The group of sculptured horses impetuously
rising from earth brilliantly symbolizes this forward-look-

ing, dynamic attitude within the modern mind. The baroque sculpture still expresses much of the vitality of our Western civilization.

Against this culture are massed its enemies, among them the chief current vulgarities and banalities. In a metaphor with double-edged meaning, the poet deplores "The throstle on the gramophone," by which it is inferred that our musical culture rests on bad naturalistic compositions heard over poor mechanical instruments. (Stevens may well have been thinking of early recordings of Respighi's "Pines of Rome.") Although our material betterment is undeniable, offering, perhaps, two ducks for dinner in place of one, and two cars in each garage, in our rapidly changing mechanized society the destiny of our culture lies too far beyond our guidance. Even the most imaginative man can with difficulty conceive the course of this bewildering social change. Genius proves inadequate for the hour but as yet is not wholly defeated. "A Duck for Dinner" ends with at least qualified hope for civilization's future.

The powerful final section of "Owl's Clover," "Sombre Figuration," enters at once upon a darker mood than "A Duck for Dinner," and concludes in a mood quite opposite to that of the relatively hopeful preceding section. This should not indicate that Stevens is himself confirmed in pessimism, but only that for artistic purposes he prefers to give his poem a somber ending, a tragic fall, without the spiritual recuperation that classical tragedy demands. His entire poem tends toward the somberly satirical. Aesthetically it seems right that it should end in darkness. The world as he here envisages it is not conceived as a comedy; art yearns toward no divine apocalypse; and even the marble horses must in the end come to dust. If the poem on civilization is to reach an absolute finality, this finality must in all honesty be tragedy.

The prophetic nature of Part Five largely explains the general title of the poem, "Owl's Clover." In mythology the owl is not only the bird of wisdom but of prophecy. He is a wise old bird, who knows both past and future. His age insures his knowledge of the former; his piercing vision insures his knowledge of the latter. As we have noted in examining others of his poems, Stevens also associated the owl with poetic inspiration, perhaps because with a second sight the owl flies with special assurance in the dark, thus signifying poetic intuitions. And doubtless Stevens further associated the owl with poetry because in his eyes poetry is concerned with thought no less than with beauty. Stevens later repeated the symbol in his remarkable poem on "modern death," "The Owl in the Sarcophagus." Owl's Clover is a popular name for several American wild flowers. As weeds in the field they are enjoyed by the wise owls, much as our sordid modern predicament with its historical setting is subject matter for our satirical poets.

"Sombre Figuration" exudes irony and much artifice. Stevens, firmly believing in the pragmatic exercise of reason though acknowledging no ultimate sanction for its conclusions, here describes modern thought largely in terms of the psychologist's discovery of the unconscious —"the subman," "the man below." "We have grown weary of the man that thinks," he declares; "he thinks and it is not true." Without categorical comment, Stevens declares that we have put our trust in this "subman," surrendering to phantasms, to irrational, uncontrollable forces. Thinking becomes a vague fluidity and dreams supplant thought. Dogmatisms of an Augustan age are irrevocably gone. Our art dissolves into a mist. Poetry becomes the bastard of music and music the mere lawlessness of sound. Stevens' landscape grows increasingly bleak as his poem progresses.

Abruptly a "portent" looms over the horizon. Although the poet prefers to leave its meaning vague, it is clearly the symbol and threat of the collapse not only of Western civilization but of any imagined civilization on earth. The forces of darkness are conceived as conquerors. Judging from the general argument of the poem, especially as seen in Part Four, these destructive forces are the deadening weight of an overmechanized society, the tendency of the crowd to overwhelm the imaginative men who might conceivably be its leaders, and the rapid degeneration of romantic thought leading at last to the victory of the "subman" over the hero or the "major man," with the triumph of a bastard neoprimitivism over the enlightened forces in civilization. The hope fitfully extended in Part Four of a triumph for the horses of imagination (Stevens may owe a debt for his imagery here to William Blake) is completely negated. Civilization is described as having lost its religion, which is equivalent to saying that it has lost its faith in itself and life. Conditions are inimical or even prohibitory to the rise of a valid art. Dwelling in his miasmal state, the man who has surrendered to the subman cannot know himself.

Stevens would by no means approve Delmore Swartz's aphorism that "in dreams begin responsibilities." He conceives civilization as the refinement of consciousness, not as its negation or the surrender of the refined consciousness to the formlessness of dreams. The truth of man is not, he holds, to be discerned in this jejune fashion. Art probes reality with quite other tools and in another spirit. We are faced with a generation that does not know itself because it has mistaken the means to such knowledge and mistaken the metaphysical foundations upon which sound art must rest. Man has lost his true humanity. Today and for his future days he reaps the follies of his past. The errors that are undoing him have long been stored up in misguided romantic thinking on politics, religion, philosophy, psychology, aesthetics. The cloud has gathered a great darkness and the deluge will presently fall. We approach a time when no one will desire the fruits of the imagination and when the aesthetic imagination will itself become extinct. This is our hidden desire, a spiritual suicide of the race. Materialism in league with obscurantism, the materialism of the crowd, the obscurantism of its blind leaders, unite to create an uncreative society seeking only the most vulgar and obvious physical pleasures and amusements. Mankind writes *finis* to his civilization.

Whatever may be the error or the truth of this tragic vision, no serious doubt exists that it was poetically worth creating. It delights the imagination, as the parallel conclusion of Pope's *Dunciad* delights it, and to a far greater degree stimulates thought. This is poetic thought in that it is almost infinitely suggestive, not dogmatic thought, which insists upon its single conclusion. "Sombre Figuration" is satirical and intellectual poetry of a high order, with the density of modern poetic idiom brought to its fullest fruition. The poetry is difficult only because each syllable carries so much weight; it is neither meaningless nor wilfully obscure. Stevens here can hardly be accused of the surfeit of artifice or wit sometimes said to mar his earlier verses in *Harmonium*. Image and thought, eloquence and poetry, are at last completely and harmoniously united.

XIII : *The Owl Examines the Future*

W HEN considered in all its parts, "Owl's Clover" suggests some final questions regarding Stevens' art.
Was he wise in writing as he did, in a style so compressed,
so involved, so rich in overtones, so amply endowed with
both intellectual subtlety and elusive moods, that commentaries such as the preceding on "Owl's Clover," or,
indeed, any of the commentaries in this book seem helpful and justified? The answer must, I think, be largely in
the affirmative but can be neither simple nor categorical.
To be sure, so far as Stevens was personally concerned,
the question can be met promptly and with complete assurance. He could do nothing else. His spirit was wholly
committed to his style as well as to his theme. He was
actually compelled to write in this manner and, moreover, conditions of our times have forced at least some
such style upon a large number of writers. He obviously
excelled in these experimental ventures. Whether he will
prove to have been a pioneer in paths relatively new and
not a little strange, and destined in a few decades to become smooth, acceptable, widely traveled and admired,

no one can foresee with confidence. But that he will remain a major poet, in his own terms a "major man," holding a place in American literature at least comparable to Gongora's in Spanish or Donne's in English, appears a very fair possibility. For a generation, in critical eyes his stature has been steadily growing. A momentum seems already established that should maintain his name on materially greater heights for several generations to come.

Perhaps a general view of Stevens can best be obtained by studying him in relation to an illustrious contemporary and, I believe, a poet of approximately equal stature. In relation to Yeats his distinctive qualities appear most clearly. Like Yeats, he is equally remarkable for his use of tradition and for sensitivity to the modern temper. Like Yeats also he is more noteworthy for craftsmanship than for the development of his ideas. Yet vast differences loom between them. Unlike Stevens, Yeats is impelled to mysticism, with its theistic involvements and its roots in the traditional thought of southern Asia, and to a violent emotional eroticism, with its far-flung romantic associations. Violence and intense struggle characterize all Yeats' thinking, with its further incitements from Ossianic legend and the more legitimate elements of folklore. His verse-plays reach at times a barbaric vehemence. Stevens, on the contrary, is suave, sophisticated, and aristocratic. One suggests the fires from which the other issues as the finest porcelain. Whereas Yeats shows the scars of a life seared by Dublin's revolutionary turmoil, Stevens looks with keen vision on a world torn by world wars, but from the distance of a contemplative calm. While Yeats lived in a continual equinoctial storm, Stevens stood at an elevation above the storms from which all climates and all seasons are visible. Although the art of one is the more moving, that of the other is the more civilized. Each produces a highly finished art though aware that it reflects a sadly unfinished world. But the personal world of the one is excessively raw; that of the other is distinguished by a remarkable ripeness and serenity. The house of poetry has many mansions, or, to translate the word into its modern equivalent, many rooms. The rooms of Yeats and Stevens promise many visitors for long to come.

The symbolism in "Owl's Clover" itself suggests, however, a more detailed and discriminating answer to the question of Stevens' place in literary history than any advanced so far. The confidence that one feels in his work can be summarily explained, and with the aid of his own suggestions. His symbol in "Owl's Clover" of the horses at the same time pressing the ground and pawing the air, denting the earth and reaching upward into the freedom of space, indicates his own position or that of virtually any other poet for whom the future holds auspicious promise. There can be no doubt that his horses, as Stevens describes them, are of the baroque era, deriving from the inspiration of Bernini. They belong in one sense to time past. Yet in Part Four of "Owl's Clover" Stevens conceives their attitude of aspiration as symbolical of a forward movement in modern art, for all sound art is by definition modern in being fresh, inventive, and oriented toward the future. Above all, in our own times the speed at which civilization moves demands this. Stevens is himself to a most extraordinary degree Janus-faced, both a traditionalist and an experimenter. A friend and advocate of modern art in many forms, of Picasso and of leading contemporary composers, he is also an apologist for classical art and for

Virgil. Almost every major artist is a colossus bridging past and future. Stevens is a supremely eloquent champion of tradition, which, as he conceives it, preserves both art and civilization from the fires of barbarism, as Aeneas carried his father, Anchises, on his shoulders out of burning Troy. As Stevens envisages the problem of permanence and change, whatever art is truly sound and potent for its own times possesses the strength to become classical for a long period to come. Not, as Book Five of "Owl's Clover" reminds us, for all time, but for a relatively long time as history conceives it. This best describes his own ambivalent position as far as one may at present judiciously appraise it. His art, like that of Yeats, combines the dignity of an honored past with the vitality of a dynamic future. It always leaned forward, moving in the vanguard of contemporary literature, exhibiting qualities fresh, invigorating, new. What can be more alive or modern than his own poem on "modern death," "The Owl in the Sarcophagus"? The element of optimism in his view of both art and life should not be underestimated here. His work as a whole can by no means be described as a typical product of a currently popular waste land, a dusty graveyard in malodorous decay. On the contrary, he proclaims both human dignity and the almost incredible beauty and dignity of the universe in which man finds himself. This heroic element in Stevens suggests once more the accomplishment of Yeats. There is strength here, both in Stevens' art and in his philosophy, suggesting the hardness of Pentelic marble. And like marble outlined by Attic sunlight, his works will last a long while before, as he himself soberly reminds us, they fall into the common dust from which all things rise.

Index

INDEX OF NAMES

INDEX OF POEMS

The following is an index of poems by Wallace Stevens referred to in this book. References to the chief commentaries on the poems are in italics.